Church *in* Crisis

Church *in* Crisis

The Gay Controversy and the Anglican Communion

OLIVER O'DONOVAN

CASCADE *Books* · Eugene, Oregon

CHURCH IN CRISIS
The Gay Controversy and the Anglican Communion

Cascade Books
A Division of Wipf and Stock Publishers
199 W. 8th Ave., Suite 3
Eugene, OR 97401

www.wipfandstock.com

ISBN 13: 978-1-55635-897-5

Cataloging-in-Publication data:

O'Donovan, Oliver

    Church in crisis : the gay controversy and the Anglican communion. / Oliver O'Donovan.

    x + 124 p. ; 23 cm. —Includes bibliographical references

    ISBN 13: 978-1-55635-897-5

    1. Homosexuality—Religious aspects—Anglican Communion. 2. Anglican Communion—Doctrines. 3. Anglican Communion—Doctrines—Sermons. I. Title.

BX5005 .O36 2008

Manufactured in the U.S.A.

CONTENTS

PREFACE

THE SEVEN CHAPTERS of this book were originally published at monthly intervals between June 2006 and January
2007 on the London-based Fulcrum Web site under the partly
ironic title, "Sermons on the Subject of the Day," borrowed
from Newman's last published collection in the Church of
England. They were never sermons in the proper sense of the
word, but polemical essays, contributions to the now long-
running struggle of the Anglican Communion for its future
existence, a struggle that entered its latest and possibly mortal
phase with the consecration of a gay divorcé as bishop of the
Diocese of New Hampshire in 2003, but which can be seen
to have been in preparation for years previously. Events have
moved fast since these pieces were written, and for up-to-the-
minute event-watchers, they will have the feel of the day before yesterday. Moments of hope and moments of despair have
come and gone. The task of drafting an Anglican Covenant is
well under way, and now we are on the threshold of the 2008
Lambeth Conference, which will certainly mark a point of no
return for better or worse. The reason for putting them now

in this more accessible form is that the diagnosis they present still seems to me persuasive. Certain older assumptions and ways of coping that served Anglicans well in the past have now failed. Nothing will do but that we bend our minds to the task of thinking deeply together, asking basic and open-ended questions about the challenges we face and the authority we acknowledge.

Prompted by a reminiscence of that earlier crisis in Anglican identity that evoked a book from Newman, the designation of these essays as "sermons" was ironic, but also hopeful. Even church polemics, unpleasant a form of communication as they are, can be, and at moments of need sometimes have been, elevated to achieve the effect of good preaching, setting stubborn issues within a new and more radically Christian framework, to be addressed in a spirit of evangelical faith and hope. I am well aware that it is difficult to align the polemical aim with the homiletic one. Only, perhaps, as criticisms are seen to bear upon all and encouragement to exclude nobody, can they transcend the incessant exchange of misunderstanding and misrepresentation. And that is what is done when the cross and resurrection of Christ are faithfully preached. The reader alone can judge how close I have come to achieving this goal.

New College, Edinburgh
Lent 2008

ACKNOWLEDGEMENTS

THE AUTHOR AND publisher wish to acknowledge the leadership and generosity of Fulcrum—the network of evangelical Anglicans dedicated to renewing "the centre of the evangelical tradition and the centre of Anglicanism." Fulcrum first published these *Sermons on the Subjects of the Day* on its website: http://www.fulcrum-anglican.org.uk. We are grateful to Graham Kings for granting permission to republish them in book form.

1 THE FAILURE *of the* LIBERAL PARADIGM

*Your treaty with death will be annulled, and your pact
with Sheol will not stand.*

(Isa 29:18)

EIGHTY YEARS AGO the poet Robert Frost penned an affectionately mocking portrait of his home state: endowed with every feature and advantage, it was proud of having nothing to sell, nothing "in commercial quantities." But did it perhaps have "an idea to sell"—like the man who once tried to persuade him to write a political pamphlet in verse? No, Frost declares—unpresciently, as it now seems. "It never could have happened in New Hampshire!"[1]

In 2003 New Hampshire had an idea to sell. On all sides it was agreed, it was the *principle* of the thing. No one pleaded in defense of the consecration that, after all, the Anglican Communion could surely wink an eye at *one* gay bishop! What

---

1. Frost, *Collected Poems*, 200.

1

was on trial was quite simply a proposition: a divorcé in an active homosexual partnership may be a worthy chief pastor of a Christian flock. Two years earlier a diocese in Canada had stepped forward, probably outside its legal competence, to enact another proposition: the church may solemnize a same-sex union with a rite of blessing. In the subsequent row, the two propositions have become inextricably associated; in the future, if the Anglican Communion has a future, they will need to be disentangled again.

What was implied in the propositions? What did they mean to say about the creation of Adam and Eve, about Natural Law and history, about principle and pastoral accommodation? The difficulty was that we did not know, and still do not. They had the virtue and the weakness of all political propositions: they could be read in many ways, with different interpretations put on them and different inferences drawn from them. In defending them the North American churches followed the counsel that it was wiser not to be too explicit. They spoke to the world about a "discernment" they had been privileged to make over a long time and from the grassroots up, leaving the ontology of the question strictly to one side.[2] *The Windsor Report* thought it surprising that the actions of the Canadian and US churches were so unaccompanied by theological explanation or interpretative commentary.[3]

---

2. ECUSA presiding bishop's statement to the 2005 primates' meeting at Dromantine.

3. Lambeth Commission on Communion, *Windsor Report 2004*, 30: "Neither the Diocese of New Westminster nor the Episcopal Church (USA) has made a serious attempt to offer an explanation to, or consult meaningfully with, the Communion as a whole about the significant development of a theology which alone could justify the recent moves by a diocese or a province."

The North American initiative presaged a worldwide drought of trust and understanding in the Anglican churches, in which every spring of traditional affection seemed to dry up and the communion seemed near to death. At the Dromantine meeting of 2005, the Primates themselves declined to receive communion together. Responding to the emergency, the Primates' meetings of 2003 and 2005, together with *The Windsor Report* (2004) which they commissioned and endorsed, attempted to create a new kind of worldwide conciliar process such as Anglican churches had never had before and had never needed. It has moved painfully slowly, so slowly that some have wanted to declare it stillborn. The Archbishop of Canterbury's measured statement of June 27th, 2006, however, still showed a resolve to carry it forward in the wake of the resolutions of the 2006 General Convention of the Episcopal Church of the USA (ECUSA). As Lambeth 2008 approaches, there may be a cloud no bigger than a man's hand to be seen on the horizon. It is too early to be sure.[4]

The task these essays address is that of sketching in outline the content of a consultative endeavor still very difficult to conceive in detail. If the "miscarrying womb and dry breasts" with which Newman reproached his mother-church in his valedictory sermon, "Parting of Friends" were a rhetorical extravagance on the part of one who had lost his sense of proportion, there are plenty who, with greater or less exaggeration, repeat the charge today.[5] Can we find an answer to it? That will certainly depend on the Anglican churches' ability to sustain a disciplined common deliberation about Christian life in the world. But to pave the way for that, we must engage with the

4. Williams, "Challenge and Hope."
5. Newman, "Parting of Friends," 460–62.

situation to which the churches have come in a manner that will strike some as polemical. To sketch broad lines of opinion, to subject them to broad lines of criticism, is a rough-and-ready business at best and inevitably a contentious one. If the sketch is any good, some will see their opinions reflected in it; if it has any breadth, they will complain that justice has not been done to their subtleties. How can it be otherwise? I know no way of escaping the problem but to ask for as much charity and fairness in return as my reader may think I have offered.

For it has to be said at the beginning: the crisis in Anglican Christianity is quite specifically a crisis in its hegemonic tradition and the manner in which it has managed and controlled differences in the past. The church's old habits of negotiating stubborn oppositions by synthesizing them within a central, undogmatic stream of opinion—let us follow the convention and call the paradigm "liberal," without prejudice to any person or group claiming that title as their own—seem to have fallen away. When from as early as Queen Victoria's day British prime ministers preferred liberal bishops, it was because they seemed to be able to stop the church from falling apart; they seemed to have made a covenant with death and a pact with Sheol. They mediated effectively between antithetical dogmatic poles, catholic and evangelical, that marked the extremes of Anglican identity since the Oxford movement in the 1830s. In the late twentieth century, it began to be apparent that this traditional spectrum might be reconfigured; what the New Hampshire crisis announced was that this had finally occurred. The historically centripetal middle had become a new centrifugal pole.

Recent essays advocating a revisionist approach to homosexuality afford an interesting perspective on the present state of liberal Anglican thought.[6] It appears to be in deep denial: denial about the record of the past, denial about the traditional role of the Lambeth Conference and its authority, denial about the crisis of the present. (One theologian actually counsels us to deal according to the old proverb "If it ain't broke, don't fix it!") In deploring what the Primates have done, it offers little acknowledgment that the Anglican Communion is in sore need of doing something. There are times, of course, when it is the higher wisdom not to produce answers to every practical dilemma others thrust on us. Like a breach birth, a moral crisis may present itself from the wrong angle and need rotation before it can be brought into the daylight of a sensible answer. It may be that before the problems of the post–New Hampshire churches can be solved, a *pas en arrière* is required, a reopening of some questionable assumptions. But that defense is not available to liberals who oppose that very strategy when it is pursued by the Windsor-Dromantine process. Stepping back, untangling the skein, reconciling conflicting views, toning down exaggerated positions, forging coalitions, squaring circles, finding commonsense ways through: the whole stock in trade of a tradition once defined by opposition to enthusiasm of every kind, seems to have been mysteriously wiped off the software. In its place are radical postures, strident denunciations and moralistic confessionalism. Here we are at act 1, scene 2, on the opening night, and the production is already going badly: the scenery has collapsed; the villain has fluffed the lines that should have struck terror into the Upper Circle; the curtain has been down too long; the audience is restive. Surely it is time for the hero to appear, and the lovely heroine whose courage and beauty draw the crowds back to see the play

6. Linzey and Kirker, *Gays and the Future of Anglicanism.*

a dozen times? And where are the well-drilled extras who will keep them on the edge of their seats with a stunning display of hand-to-hand fighting? The producer looks around, nervously. Good Lord! There they are, up in the gallery, booing and cat-calling along with the audience!

Religious liberalism is not an Anglican phenomenon alone, but a pan-Protestant one. "Pan-Christian," one might say, since Roman Catholicism has had two difficult engagements with its own liberals in the course of the twentieth century, one in the early years with the so-called Modernist Controversy about historical biblical criticism, the other in the postconciliar period about the direction of moral theology. But the hegemonic character of liberalism in the Protestant churches has given it a distinctive profile, which deserves to be treated on its own terms. "Liberal" is a word with many uses, both intellectual and political, and its protean polyvalence can create misunderstanding. Political liberalism and theological liberalism are animals of a single genus but different species. When qualifying a religious posture, "liberal" suggests independence in relation to spiritual authorities—scriptural, hierarchical, or congregational. This distance may be no more than a questioning habit of mind, an independence of judgment that may lead back to a new and clarified recognition of authority. It may, on the other hand, be a deep alienation that fosters resentments which never quite proceed to an open breach. There is no way of telling a priori where on the spectrum of distance any "liberal" proposal will turn out to lie. It may be renewing; it may be subversive. The tree will be known by its fruits, and by nothing else. Yet in the lowering gloom of the Liberal Christian evening, we ought to begin by acknowledging the good that has been wrought in its day. No major theological voice of our age has failed to have its intonations deepened by what the Archbishop of Canterbury describes as its "habit of cultural sensitivity and intellectual flexibility that does not seek to close down unexpected questions too quickly."[7] For what we have received may the Lord make us truly thankful!

The story of theological liberalism could in principle be taken back a long way—certainly to the fission of the established Protestant churches in the seventeenth century, and perhaps to Renaissance humanism, even to Abelard. To understand the twentieth century, however, it makes sense to begin from the nineteenth-century attempt to reconstruct the expression of Christian doctrine by reference to ethics, the program of "the primacy of the ethical," drawn from the Ritschlian school of post-Kantian theologians in Germany. The interests of this school lay with dogma, which needed adaptation to the scientific climate of post-Enlightenment civilization. Ethics had "primacy," but only in the sense of being *presupposed*; it was the starting point of the dogmatic inquiry. To the intelligentsia of this period ethical judgments seemed very much more certain than creedal formulations. Predestination, resurrection, the omniscience and omnipotence of God, each chapter in the catechism could be interrogated as to its expression of the noblest and highest ideals, and rewritten as necessary. Ethics afforded a criterion by which the truth of doctrine could be verified: "belief in truth of a special and practical kind . . . as life-truth, in its central and creative reality for our person, and not in its congruity with other truth. . . . Christ did not come to teach us truth, but to make us true."[8] The ethical conception of truth was the essence of the modern; and this program was *ex professo* "modernist," taking for granted that the highest and noblest

7. Williams, "Challenge and Hope."
8. Forsyth, *Principle of Authority*, 4, 18.

ideals were being grasped and realized in contemporary history. Standing in no need of independent inquiry to verify them, they were immediately available to verify Christian dogma.

It has often been claimed that liberalism implied no special doctrines but was merely a critical temper of mind. This claim was never quite untrue; but it is an important aspect of our current situation that it was never quite true either. Liberalism related itself to the traditional dogmas of the church and aimed to modulate them. Inevitably, its methodology was reflected in an account of Christian belief with a distinctive shape. The inner shrine of the liberal gospel was its attitude of respectful attentiveness to the world as it is. The term "incarnation," used without an article, speaks of this embrace of the world. This is something different from *the* incarnation, the historical birth of Jesus the Son of God from Mary, which is now reconstructed as a paradigm or model for a conjunction of the human and divine to be effected in all times and places. The incarnation of the Word takes place continually. Being party to the positive conjunction of God and world is the distinct form of theosis offered to believers in liberal theology.

In making this conjunction its object, liberalism assimilated a Protestant construction of Christian existence in missiological terms. In assuming it already present and needing only to be affirmed, it assimilated a Catholic, doxological one. Yet the conception is neither Protestant nor Catholic. Both the eschatological frontier between this world and the next, important to Protestants, and the ontological frontier between the Creator and the creature, important to Catholics, are collapsed. This world being the sanctuary of God's full self-disclosure, talk of a reign of God can only be talk of this world projected to its logical term. The present harbors no ultimate antithesis; it faces no final judgment. God's worldly self-disclosure may be seen as the dynamic of world history, as in the confident progressivism of an earlier liberalism, or simply as a series of disjoined intuitions, as in the existentialism that replaced it. But one way or the other the theological liberal looks to "see the hand of the Lord in the land of the living" (Ps 27:13), and knows that when seen it will be stretched out in blessing, not in judgment.

A prime candidate for reconstruction among the classical doctrines was, of course, sin and judgment. Original sin, the understanding of the human world as lying as such under divine judgment, is replaced by resistance to mediation and reconciliation, tardiness over the opportunities of the present; judgment as the destiny of this world is replaced by a patience of divinity that can outwait the longest delaying tactic. And here we encounter one of those important, but possibly misleading, intersections of theological liberalism with the political stance bearing the same name. "Sin is conservatism" is a thesis on which the two liberalisms could converge. Yet their approaches to the common thesis are actually quite different. "Conservative," for the political liberal, designates a determinate social order, authoritarian and nonreciprocal, inhibiting individual initiative and freedom, which merely happens to have prevailed at some point in the past; if the ebb and flow of history were to yield a new flood tide for such an order, the political liberal would resist it just the same. For the theological liberal, on the other hand, the substantive content is indeterminate, and what is wrong with conservatism is precisely that it clings to the past, holding back in reserve from the God-destined character of the present cultural moment. At which point the distinctive character of liberal ecclesiology comes into view; for what can it be that holds us back, if not the stubborn antithesis of church and world? The self-validating ethical convictions of modern civilization are the final criterion for judging all else; they are the very image of God that it bears anonymously as its birthright. Resistance to the image of God may come from any source, but most typically it comes from where the antithesis is most upheld, which is to say, the church. All that is institutional and naturally sluggish about the church is a standing problem, a regressive obstacle in the way of its incarnational mission. Ecclesiology begins and ends with the *semper reformanda,* the casting off of the fossilized deposit of an outworn past.

Of this thumbnail doctrinal sketch it will rightly be said that it shares the limitations of all thumbnail sketches. It represents an "ideal type," tending to caricature and corresponding precisely to the views of no one in particular. When this is conceded, however, it can play a useful heuristic role; it can help us diagnose the problem that has drained the hegemonic tradition of its strength. For there certainly has been strength in the program of reviewing doctrine critically in the light of ethics. Hopeful attention to the present as the theater of God's action has proved to be an absorbent and reconciling catalyst. Liberal thought in Anglicanism has woven itself in and through other strands of thought, balancing and qualifying angular postures and attitudes and so negotiating institutional Anglicanism's self-effacing way through the world. When the thread was strong, it knit the church together. Why, then, did it snap? Was it because of a one-sided emphasis on reason, as critics have often said? Did it promote rationalism rather than faith seeking understanding?

My own analysis is rather different. If the antecedent for the program of the "primacy of the ethical" is Kantian, it is not the Kant of the *second* critique, the critique of practical reason, into which liberalism never really ventured. Here lies the point of truth in the accusation that liberalism, far from being over-serious about reason, treats it "all too blithely."[9] If it is necessary for reason to think the true in the light of the good, it is no less necessary for it to think the good in the light of the true. An apriorist "intuitionism" in ethics which, as one critic has well said, "wants to know too much about values, and to know it too quickly," cuts short the disciplines of discursive practical inquiry.[10] The liberal compact with modernity was ratified in the court of Hegelian idealism, and "Hegel," as Kierkegaard already observed tartly, "had no ethic."[11] Kierkegaard's account of the downfall of poor mad Pastor Adler, persuaded by Hegelian dialectics to think of himself as a prophet, might serve as an account of the crack-up of the liberal tradition as a whole. In the interests of finding the modern world God-enchanted, it closed down on the serious deliberation with which Christians ought to weigh their stance of witness in the world. Potentially world-critical questions were suppressed. Liberal moral commitments, though sometimes urged with a passion verging on outright moralism, were not steered from the helm of discursive inquiry but set adrift on the moral currents of the day.

Among the early passages of arms between the sinking catholic and rising liberal powers in the second decade of the twentieth century, one minor but interesting one is recorded by Hastings Rashdall, a liberal of some note as a moral philosopher. "I was requested to give evidence before the Royal Commission," he wrote, "which has recently been investigating the question of the Divorce Laws in England. I ventured to suggest that the question was one upon which the moral consciousness had

9. I borrow the happy phrase from Benedict XVI. See Ratzinger, "Church's Teaching: Authority, Faith, Morals," 52.

10. Lacoste, "Du phénomène de la valeur au discours de la norme," 123.

11. Kierkegaard, *On Authority and Revelation*, 129.

something to say. Thereupon I was severely cross-examined by eminent ecclesiastical authorities as though I were a setter forth of strange gods . . ."[12] And from the vantage point of nearly a century later, one can only comment that Rashdall's gods look very strange indeed. *The* moral consciousness? By what right does the definite article, carefully detached from the incarnation, attach itself to the collective moral judgments of the human race? Are we to listen out for a single decisive judgment of the human conscience, so pronounced and so unanimous that only crabbed churchmen and cantankerous academics will dare raise questions about it? That is a pretty remote proposition for the world that has come to supervene in the past ninety years! Here, as often, the conservatives of a past age had greater premonitions of the deeper currents, since they were more skeptical about the shallow eddies. That the twentieth century saw the recovery of a discipline of ethics in the Anglican theological tradition (absent more or less since the seventeenth century) was due not to liberal but to Catholic impulses. [13]

The relation of liberal Christianity to the modern world, then, contains a paradox. Turning, as all Christianity must, from contemplation of past and transcendent realities to consider how it must behave, it orients itself to a present world

---

12. Rashdall, *Conscience and Christ,* 5

13. The story deserves quotation as a moment full of symbolism for the transition of an age: Rashdall's was the ecclesiastically rising star, but intellectually his style of moral philosophy was at the end of its influence, while the work of my Oxford predecessor Kenneth Kirk still lay in the future. One should, however, quote it with a frank admission that it hardly does justice to Rashdall's contribution. Can we keep our anger forever against someone who was prepared to devote such careful attention to the moral teaching of Jesus of Nazareth—even if he seriously imagined himself (and everyone else) capable of estimating its true worth by the inner illumination of a moral a priori?

that has its primary meaning as *our* task, the challenge to *our* action. (That is the primary meaning of the present for us who live in it, at any rate; what meaning it may have for our grandchildren, who will look back on it as their past, is not ours to comprehend.) Yet liberalism fails to bring a critical practical reason to bear on the present world. In its pursuit of doctrinal reconstruction, it treats the moral questions of the age as moral certainties; it views the indeterminate shapes of the present as sharp outlines. It may even imagine that in the present it can find some kind of speculative counterweight to correct a bias in past and transcendent reality. Instead of looking to the world as a frame within which to serve God and neighbor, it looks to it for a demonstration that in the past reality was misunderstood. Thus is crystallized the "modern world," an artificial entity with no existence in real time, achieving its dominion over thought only as we allow the world of *action*, for which we should have our loins girded ready for adventure, to be permafrosted into a world of pseudo-fact.

The tragic fault of liberal Christianity was to have no critical purchase on moral intuitions comparable to the purchase it had on doctrinal judgments. Precisely for that reason liberalism proved vulnerable when twentieth-century society began to be riven through with deep moral fissures. In affirming the world, liberal theology condemned itself to shipwreck on the same rocks where a unified modern civilization broke up. Decolonialization left it without a dominant moral tradition that it could claim as forerunner of the kingdom of God. When economic self-interest and the emancipation of the senses became the solvent forces of the new West, unhappy Christian liberals struggled to keep the smile on their faces and suppress their instinctive repulsion. Comparatively late in the story, the tradition of theological liberalism reached for narratives of emancipation to give its cause fresh energy.

The older political-liberal narratives told the story of Western history as a story of constitutional complexification, dissolution of privilege, taming of autocratic government, and the economic and political equalization of the classes. Their tone was complacent and gradualist. It was the postwar conflict with communism that first imparted a crusading note to political liberalism. As though to drown out the revolutionary trumpets of the East, Western society began to proclaim itself the site of an ongoing series of conflicts over sectional emancipations and inclusions. It was natural that this style of civilizational apologetics should have an appeal for Christians. There were some very good stories of emancipation to be told, testimonies to the liberating implications of the gospel and the pastoral involvement of the church, the enormously influential struggle for civil rights in the USA, for instance, and the Latin American base ecclesial communities that gave new sharpness to Catholic witness in the face of poverty and economic injustice. These threw a lifeline to a floundering liberal imagination, offering a matrix by which the present could be seen as standing in perpetual judgment on the past, allowing the Western hegemonic tradition of modernity to rebrand its anticonservative appeal. Whether the pastoral and missionary endeavors that inspired this rebranding were helped forward by being put to this use, is a question we may leave aside. In grasping the lifeline, however, Western liberalism paid its price. From that point on, it became identified with one kind of moral cause to the exclusion of others. It became a church-party proper, a specific agenda to pit against other agendas.

Whether, if prevailing fashions of thought had been different, the emergent gay consciousness would have presented itself to the church as an excluded class in search of inclusion, is not a question it is possible to answer. What does deserve comment, however, is a persistent lack of fit between what gays find important about themselves and the role they are given to play in the emancipatory narrative. Gays do not always present themselves as natural liberals, since they represent a sectional rather than a universal vision. The *specialness* of gay experience is important to them. It was an insight into this logic that led the late Michael Vasey to insist that the natural discussion partners for gays who took their own experience seriously were Christians of a more conservative stamp, for whom sex was also a matter of interest as such.[14] The gay cause is grist for the liberal mill while it is in militant mode, for the mill processes victim classes in want of a fair deal. But Proudhon's "Justice, nothing but justice!" is as restrictive on one front as it is empowering on the other.[15] It allows not the slightest observation on the aesthetic or emotional timbre of gay existence. To demand justice is to make this class like every other class, for justice is thought's weapon against arbitrariness. But when gay experience starts attracting interest and interrogation in its own right and for its own sake, its usefulness to the liberal project is at an end. For that raises questions that were supposed to have been settled long ago; it draws attention to the fragmentation of the modern moral world, and therefore to its insufficiency as a measure to judge the performance of the church.

Gays also pose existential questions. They interest themselves in the riddle of gay existence. *Anexetastos bios abiôtos*, said Socrates; the life that is unexamined is intolerable to live. And much of the gay angst is to do with the difficulty of raising

14. See Vasey, *Strangers and Friends*.
15. Proudhon, *What Is Property?* 15.

questions in public that seem overwhelmingly pressing when they directly concern oneself. The pastoral challenge that the gay phenomenon presents to the church, then, is not primarily emancipatory, but hermeneutic. And that is the supreme justification for a conciliar process that will take up the experience of homosexual Christians as its leading question. How is this form of feeling to be understood? What are the patterns of life with which it may appropriately clothe itself? As far as I can tell, it is deeply in the interest of gay Christians, men and women, that their experience—by which is meant not merely *sexual* experience, not merely *emotional* experience, and not merely the *narrative* of experience, but the whole storehouse of what they have felt and thought about their lives, should become a matter of wider reflection, reflected on by those who are called to live this experience, by those who are called to accompany them in their living, by all who share their understanding of living as something they owe an account of to God.

Ten years ago an abortive attempt was made to open such a discussion by the authors—antirevisionist in their assumptions—of the "St. Andrew's Day Statement."[16] Various aspects of the document ensured that its intentions were not well understood: its confessional structure, meant to provide an ecumenical rather than sectarian framework, deterred those more used to experience-based discussions; its reticence in saying things it wanted to treat as secondary encouraged critics triumphantly to uncover what the "real" point was, and so on.[17]

16. See "St. Andrew's Day Statement," in Bradshaw, *Way Forward?* 5–11.

17. Foreseeing their risk of this fate, the authors hoped to avert it by warning readers not to read "between the lines." That, however, is where current fashions of "unmasking" have taught a whole generation of readers to begin and end their reading!

What remains important about the attempt, however, was that it addressed questions quite specifically *to gay Christians,* not to liberals, and *about the essentials of Christian faith.* Long as the way might seem, these authors thought there was an exploration to be had, which, if undertaken in good faith, might yield a common discussion over what it could mean to be both homosexual and Christian. It appeared that Christian gays were not prepared for that discussion at that time. Fruitful gay self-interrogations in the secular world had not yet prompted gay believers to embark on a comparable course. What is the situation today? Is the gay Christian movement still attached to the wheels of the liberal chariot, content with the victim mentality that the liberal program prescribes for it? Or can it present itself as the bearer of an experience of the human that is, at the very least, of irreplaceable importance for our understanding of our own times? Is it of age, able to speak for itself? On the answer to that a great deal may depend.

2 THE CARE
of the CHURCHES

And apart from other things there is the daily pressure
on me of my anxiety for all the churches.

(2 Corinthians 11:28)

AT THE STILL center of the storm in the Anglican Communion stands the isolated, scholarly figure of the current
Archbishop of Canterbury—the first holder of that office since
the Reformation, it is worth recalling, to have come to it directly from outside the Church of England, and probably the
only one to have received appointment by something close to
acclamation. It is necessary to recall the circumstances.

In 2001, on the verge of the British-American invasion
of Iraq, the British prime minister must surely have had some
qualms about placing in the seat of highest spiritual authority in
England a figure known both for antiwar and disestablishment
sympathies. (His theological credentials as a critic of liberalism were, perhaps, less in the prime minister's mind.) Popular
demand in England for the appointment of the reluctant

Archbishop of Wales was, however, widespread, and embraced all the traditional party emphases. This harmony was disturbed at the last minute by a vigorous press campaign in his favor in the pro-gay interest, signaling an expectation in some quarters that he would promote a change of attitude on the subject; this produced a panicky reaction of hostility from some evangelicals. But most, even of these, knew well enough that the press portrait of the "radical" Archbishop revealed only a fraction of the sympathies of a complex mind, and reckoned that he would make it his first business at Canterbury to seek a common judgment and pursue a common policy. The lengthy personal statement of June 27th, 2006, confirms what was evident from the beginning: that the Archbishop's own comportment in relation to the crisis is indissolubly identified with the conciliar policy of Windsor and Dromantine. And that is not the least cause of his present isolation, for conciliarity has been his practice, not merely his theory, at a time when many have wanted high-profile personal gestures. Such gestures used not to lie outside his repertoire: his appointment to the Lady Margaret Professorship at Oxford was greeted by John Macquarrie, his predecessor, with the unforgettable words, "He'll do fine—if he's out of jail at the time!" But they do lie outside his very Anglican understanding of church authority. "The idea of an Archbishop of Canterbury resolving any of this by decree," he writes, "is misplaced, however tempting for many. The Archbishop of Canterbury presides and convenes in the Communion, and may . . . outline the theological framework in which a problem should be addressed; but he must always act collegially, with the bishops of his own local Church and with the Primates and other instruments of communion."[1]

---

1. Williams, "Challenge and Hope."

The Anglican Communion was not the first major family of churches to be caught up in the throes of a divisive moral disagreement; the Roman Catholic Church after Humanae Vitae found itself in just such a state of disarray. In that case, however, the ecclesiological tools needed to confront the disagreement lay to hand; for the Anglicans they did not. The most important feature of The Windsor Report was an attempt to forge them. The serendipitous character of Windsor's achievement was to combine the somewhat ill-defined commitment of the 1998 Lambeth Conference to an ongoing "listening" to homosexual Christians' experience with a project for which the churches of the Southern hemisphere were eager, "mending the nets," i.e., constitutional reform of the Communion's institutions that would have the effect of weakening Northern, and especially US influence. A surprising amount of Windsor's attention was given to longer-term prescriptions for what it called the "instruments of unity," i.e., the primacy of Canterbury, the Primates' meeting, the Anglican Consultative Council. and the Lambeth Conference, including the proposal of a common canon-law framework to define their roles. This caused some dismay among Northern Hemisphere Anglicans, which might have shipwrecked the proposals from the outset; but it also tended to win the confidence of the churches of the South, more likely to be suspicious or lassitudinous about the listening process.

Windsor looked to find a point of reference in ecclesiology, borrowing aspects of the "communion ecclesiology" elaborated in Anglican-Roman Catholic discussion. The irony of this should not pass without notice. The historic stress lines of the Anglican self-consciousness were ecclesiological; yet at the beginning of the twenty-first century the one point offering some hope of purchase on an intractable disagreement was a doctrine of the church worked out in conversations with ecumenical partners. Almost everything else that might have served as a point of reference was in contention: the ethical a prioris to which liberalism habitually appealed; the authority and hermeneutic of Scripture, to which evangelicals appealed. More than an irony, it was in its way a triumph: a triumph for the ecumenical movement from an unlikely source, and even, since the ecumenical movement itself owed much of its early impetus to liberal antidogmatism, a triumph for the liberal hegemony of the century just closed. Yet antidogmatism alone could not have produced communion ecclesiology, and at the close of the twentieth century liberal Christianity, increasingly suspicious of doctrinal agreement, by no means looked on the ecumenical movement as its favorite child. Another case of Newman's "miscarrying womb," perhaps?

For one church to wish it of another "that you may have communion with us" is framed by a daring and demanding conviction: "our communion is with the Father and with his Son Jesus Christ" (1 John 1:3). No communion can possibly be claimed within the church of Christ on other than these gospel terms. But to claim evangelical communion is a statement of faith in God's gift of himself, a gift that cannot be proved empirically, but must be believed in and witnessed to. In the divided state of the Christian churches, no witness to it will be perfect. Yet it is not unwitnessed to. Ecumenical encounters between the churches witness to it; so do attempts to make existing institutions and structures more serviceable within the churches. What makes a structure serviceable? It is serviceable when it secures communion within the church on its gospel basis; for "one holy, catholic and apostolic church" cannot live apart from "one faith" and "one baptism." In order to do this, structures must be equipped to exercise judgment, to draw a line, where necessary, between true and false communion. To have structures capable of doing that is to enjoy an institutional communion that witnesses to, and safeguards, evangelical communion.

Evangelical communion is never merely synchronic; it is always also diachronic, involving a communion with past Christians in receiving from them the faith they have witnessed to and handing that faith on again to further generations. This is what is meant when we speak of the need to preserve "tradition." Traditional communion does not imply that there can be no radical correction of the tradition as received, such as was undertaken in the Reformation. Tradition is founded upon the authority of the prophets' and apostles' testimony to Christ, and so has a principle of self-correction built into it with the authority of Scripture. It does imply, however, that when there is a question about authentic terms of communion, tradition has a significant role in helping us answer it. Anglicans have understood the authority of tradition as running much wider and deeper than what has been thought and done by Anglicans. They have aimed to interpret and regulate Anglican practices in the light of an ecumenical tradition running back to the apostolic age.

Only in this wider context can the role of the instruments of unity within the Communion be understood. The significance of the See of Canterbury, in particular, lies in its service to the tradition of Christian faith and practice. The Archbishop has authority; but, like all authority, his is subject to the authority of God the Holy Spirit speaking to and through the churches in the process of faithful receiving and transmission of tradition. It is not invested with discretion to abolish existing terms of communion and replace them with others. And what the Archbishop cannot do, neither can others by using communion with his office as a kind of wrench to split the church apart from its historic practices. "Communion with the See of

Anglican Ecclesiology

Canterbury" is an institutional function in the service of communion among Anglicans, and, through them, in the service of the communion of the *una sancta catholica ecclesia*. A claim that someone is in communion with Canterbury is not valid merely by being asserted, nor even by the acceptance of the Archbishop of the day. Such a claim must be open to evaluation, submitted to the theological test of whether the Anglican tradition of Christian faith and practice has in fact been sustained and renewed by the communion that is claimed. Just as Christians are not admitted as Christians by other Christians, only recognized as Christians on the basis of the Holy Spirit's work in them, so it is with Anglicans—for being an Anglican is simply a specific modulation of being a Christian. The heart of the Archbishop's role in the Communion is to give voice and effect to judgments the churches have reached about the work of the Spirit in their midst, to speak and act on behalf of their common mutual recognition. This is complicated by his special role within the Church of England, for the Anglican Communion is constructed on the historic relationship of its member churches to the English mother church, its senior primacy vested in the primate of all England. But that does not give the Church of England a deciding voice in defining the Communion's direction. The historic relation between the English church and the Communion is entrusted to the harmonious way the Archbishop exercises his authority in the two concentric spheres.

One way of describing the focus of the Windsor Commission is to say that it was asked to render a service to the exercise of *episkopē* within the Anglican churches, not a service of *didachē*, the teaching of the word. Its more immediate prescriptions, then, were aimed at achieving the minimum steps backward necessary to get a conciliar process on the road, a process within which the *didachē* of the church could be examined, refined, and strengthened. Minimum steps, however, did not mean "minor steps," especially in the case of the North American churches, which were asked to accept responsibility and express regret for initiating the disruption, "breaching the proper constraints of the bonds of affection" as it was portentously expressed, in the consecration of the New Hampshire bishop. The non-American bishops, on the other hand, who had intervened in the North American churches in reaction, were to express regret for the unfortunate consequences of their response to the challenge. To these proposals of the Windsor Report the Primates gave flesh in their Dromantine meeting in 2005. The heart of the action they took there was not their decision to request that ECUSA and the Anglican Church of Canada (ACC) voluntarily withdraw from the bodies of the Communion "up to the next Lambeth Conference." That was only intelligible when set beside the preceding resolution: "In order for the recommendations of The Windsor Report to be properly addressed, time needs to be given to [ECUSA and ACC] for consideration . . . according to their constitutional processes."[2] In other words, the Primates intended to begin the conciliar process in the churches that had made it necessary, allowing these churches to be heard to speak as a whole—lay, clerical, and episcopal—apart from the decisions of their leaders. It was a daring strategy, which may yet turn out to have led nowhere, depending how the ambiguous resolutions of the ECUSA General Convention finally appear on consideration. But it opened the way to those North American Anglicans who believed the measures taken were right in principle to reevaluate their policy of "never explain, never apologize," and it opened

2. Communiqué February 2005 §13. Cf. §14.

the door to those who believed the new steps misconceived to turn from impotent protest to serious synodical argument.

Shrewd observers have remarked that the Primates' response transformed a polarized situation, revisionist against antirevisionist, into a quadrant of views, where conciliarists of different judgments over the moral issue had to come to terms with anticonciliar revisionists and anticonciliar antirevisionists. The emergence of a strong conciliar front, more or less the official position of the Communion and most of its constituent churches, was what the process was supposed to achieve. An anticonciliar revisionist resistance loyal to the North American initiatives was only to be expected. But the emergence of an antirevisionist strand of opinion that was cool, to say the least, about the conciliar process was, perhaps, more perplexing. With the North Americans on the back foot, it might have seemed that antirevisionist sentiment only had to cling tight to the conciliar project. How is this development to be accounted for?

By a conjunction of two factors: the first was a confidence in the immediacy of moral judgments, such as underlay, also, the development of liberal Christianity. Where there seems to be nothing to discuss, there can be no discussion. But "in the beginning is the half-light," as one philosopher says about the foundations of ethics.[3] A process of moral reasoning is needed if we are to reach well-founded concrete moral judgments. By its very logic moral intuitionism will be indifferently radical or conservative. Once the moment of moral insight is detached from the discursive project of reflection and deliberation, it can rebound off the wall at any angle whatever. The intuitionist appeal to a "discernment" on the revisionist side called forth an equal and opposite move—all the more so since an antire-

3. Lacoste, "Du phénomène de la valeur au discours de la norme," 124.

visionist "discernment" could claim, with much greater prima facie plausibility, to be in line with the unwavering testimony of Scripture. To some reflections on how Scripture is to be approached in this discussion we must return later. It is enough to remark in passing that, on this side as on that, the immediacy of the insight tends to make the interpretation of Scripture seem superfluous. The contrast with the rather careful hermeneutic of scriptural teaching on divorce and remarriage is striking; to this interesting, if teasing analogy, too, we must return.

But there was a second cause that reinforced the intuition-Scripture conjunction. That was an interest in communion structures, the "mending the nets" agenda that had reacted in wrath to the challenge to the authority of Lambeth. This quite separate cause of offence went back to the unhappy inconclusiveness of the 1988 Conference's reflections on the consecration of women bishops, when churches supportive of that initiative made it plain that the authority of the Conference was not, in their view, sufficient to prevent it. This was a new theme in the Anglican fugue, and one with serious implications, just at the point when bishops from the developing world had achieved a majority in the Conference. In the postcolonial era, racism is necessarily a sensitive issue. The innovating churches not only failed to appreciate the wider resonances of their tough-minded pitch of 1988; some of them came back in 1998 apparently resolved to repeat the offense. Those who claim special powers of moral discernment can hardly afford such moments of massive insensitivity, to which a great deal of the bitterness is attributable. Certainly it accounts for strands of opinion that have wanted to ram the Lambeth Conference Resolution forcefully down the revisionists' throats. Hooker's *causa finita est* has been invoked in support of the view that, Lambeth having spoken, nothing remains to be said.

Yet a reading of Resolution 1.10 of Lambeth 1998—with whatever sympathy and appreciation—does not quite support the view that it was meant to bring the whole discussion to a close.[4] The attempt to treat this text as a point of closure, rather than a disciplined overture to explorations yet to be conducted, puts excessive strain on it, and tends to frustrate, not further, its goal of shaping the practices of the Communion under the authority of Scripture. It meant, certainly, to set some fairly tightly drawn parameters: faithfulness in marriage between a man and a woman in lifelong union; sexual abstinence as the

4. Let the reader judge: "This Conference: (a) commends to the Church the subsection report on human sexuality; (b) in view of the teaching of Scripture, upholds faithfulness in marriage between a man and a woman in lifelong union, and believes that abstinence is right for those who are not called to marriage; (c) recognises that there are among us persons who experience themselves as having a homosexual orientation. Many of these are members of the Church and are seeking the pastoral care, moral direction of the Church, and God's transforming power for the living of their lives and the ordering of relationships. We commit ourselves to listen to the experience of homosexual persons and we wish to assure them that they are loved by God and that all baptised, believing and faithful persons, regardless of sexual orientation, are full members of the Body of Christ; (d) while rejecting homosexual practice as incompatible with Scripture, calls on all our people to minister pastorally and sensitively to all irrespective of sexual orientation and to condemn irrational fear of homosexuals, violence within marriage and any trivialisation and commercialisation of sex; (e) cannot advise the legitimising or blessing of same sex unions nor ordaining those involved in same gender unions; (f) requests the Primates and the ACC to establish a means of monitoring the work done on the subject of human sexuality in the Communion and to share statements and resources among us; (g) notes the significance of the Kuala Lumpur Statement on Human Sexuality and the concerns expressed in resolutions IV.26, V.1, V.10, V.23 and V.35 on the authority of Scripture in matters of marriage and sexuality and asks the Primates and the ACC to include them in their monitoring process." 13th Lambeth Conference (1998), Resolution 1.10, "Human Sexuality."

right course for those not called to marriage; homosexual practice as incompatible with Scripture. At the same time it recognized the existence of church members with a homosexual orientation who were seeking pastoral care, moral direction and God's transforming power for their lives and relationships; it committed itself to a process of listening to their experience; it called for pastoral and sensitive ministry to them, but it declined to "advise the legitimising or blessing of same sex unions nor ordaining those involved in same gender unions"—the change of term may possibly mean that the pastoral problems of transsexualism were also at the back of bishops' minds. It condemned irrational fear of homosexuals, along with one or two other causes of indignation that tend to turn up at every party; it affirmed that baptized, believing, and faithful persons, regardless of sexual orientation, are full members of the Body of Christ and loved by God, and requested a means of monitoring work done on the subject of human sexuality. It was, notoriously, a resolution improvised and hammered out on the floor of a plenary session, and a variety of entertaining and only partially reconcilable narratives soon came into circulation about how the procedural debacle arose. But three things are crystal clear: it was generally conservative in posture; it was overwhelmingly supported; it was open to further exploration. And exploration must be meant to make some difference. Even if Lambeth would not envisage a major reorientation of its approach, it must have envisaged, in the light of greater pastoral experience and understanding, possibilities for considerable further nuance of detailed practice.

When The Windsor Report posed, as the alternative to its own approach, that "we shall have to begin to learn to walk apart," it clearly did not mean this as a choiceworthy alternative, one that the church of Jesus Christ could opt for with integrity.

It was to be viewed as a horizon of total failure.[5] Unhappily, it seems to have underestimated the capacity of Anglicans to think the unthinkable. The immediate effect of the hardening of the antirevisionist position was to make the breach more likely; indeed, some voices, however little representative, did not hesitate to suggest that this was something to be welcomed. On the revisionist side, the idea of an amicable separation of the ways had long been mooted—just another example of liberal otherworldliness, unfortunately, since the only separation ever to be looked for was bound to be far from amicable. To the antirevisionists looking in this direction it was to be a solemn exercise of church discipline. A curious combination of ecclesiological influences, Calvinist and patristic, had already encouraged a number of bishops to raise their voices and announce the several combinations of churches and bishops with whom they were and were not in communion. The resulting untidiness in the Anglican world communion began to make some think that a shoot-out would be the desirable curtain-fall.

But this severely underestimated its difficulties. Such an occurrence would, for one thing, destroy the Anglican identity. The Anglican churches are not, and do not claim to be the whole Christian church as comprehended in its Augsburg-derived formulae.[6] They are a particular communion of churches that mediates the gospel in a shared tradition deriving from English history and the network of global relations springing from it.

---

5. Lambeth Commission on Communion, *Windsor Report*, 75–76. Indeed, its final words, building on a statement of the 2000 Primates' meeting, embody a decisive condemnation of this option: "'to turn from one another would be to turn away from the Cross,' and indeed from serving the world which God loves and for which Christ died."

6. Thirty-Nine Articles, article 19: "The visible Church of Christ is a congregation of faithful men, in the which the pure Word of God is preached, and the Sacraments be duly administered according to Christ's ordinance. . . ."

The Anglican identity is constituted by its particular continuities, and cannot survive a decisive breach in them. Even if we were to accept this as the price to be paid for a purer church, however, there is a more profound obstacle in the way of achieving purity by these means. The new configurations could not possibly be formed along the lines of the division over homosexuality. Separating evangelicals would not carry with them all, not even perhaps the majority, of those who sympathized with their antirevisionist views. Many of their sympathizers are not evangelicals, and would certainly look for other alternatives. Many, not least evangelicals, would think such an act of separation wrong in principle. Not the new true ex-Anglicans, but the Roman Catholic Church, already recruiting evangelical intellectuals by the dozen, would be the great winners (if we can speak of winners in this dismal scenario) from the disorderly explosion of Anglican forces. The idea of a united antirevisionist Anglican church is as fantastic as the idea of an amicable parting of the ways.

The point of principle can be explored by posing the theological question: in the view of the New Testament, what grounds justify a deliberate breach in communion within the church? Two contradictory answers press themselves on us, each with apparent inevitability. On the one hand, we are never justified in breaking communion within the church of Jesus Christ, for schism is sin; on the other hand, communion implies and requires fundamental agreement in the gospel. Those who "go out" from the church of Christ declare that they were not of it (1 John 2:18). Yet disagreement is not something we are free to relativize or set to one side. So unity in the truth turns out to be a commitment that may pull us in opposite directions to opposite conclusions: there is no communion-breaking moral disagreement, on the one hand; on the other, any disagreement is potentially communion-breaking. The one answer we cannot find is the answer we set out to find: this, rather than that, is the specific cause that will justify a breach.

It is worth pausing to make a comparison with a similar moral antinomy, much discussed in the Scholastic period: Is it right to obey a mistaken conscience? On the one hand, obeying one's conscience is, apparently by definition, something it is always right to do. On the other hand, a mistaken conscience is, again by definition, a conscience that instructs you to do the wrong thing. So doing what a mistaken conscience tells you is to do right and wrong at the same time. There is a lesson to be learned from the deft way Aquinas, confronting this paradox of "perplexity," thrusts it aside. "One can withdraw from the error," he tells us.[7] Commentators have expressed bewilderment at this, for it is, of course, not an answer to the question, but an evasion. It does not tell us what to do when our conscience is mistaken; it tells us not to have a mistaken conscience. Is Aquinas merely saying, "If that was where I wanted to go, I wouldn't start from here"—always a bad answer to a practical question, since "here" is where all practical questions start from? No: he means that there is something that the framing of the question has left out of account; the alternative is wrongly posed.

It beguiles us into imagining a helpless innocent pathetically trapped between the devil of dutiful wrongdoing and the deep blue sea of guilt-ridden right-doing. Moral reality is simply not like that. The perplexed actor always has a further recourse: she or he can reconsider. The conscience is not a fixed and unnegotiable natural force, but precisely "the mind of man making moral judgments." It can therefore be made use of, and if it leads to bewildering conclusions, it can be made

7. *Summa Theologiae* II–1.19 ad 3: "potest ab errore recedere"; here, as elsewhere, unattributed translations are my own.

use of again, to reflect on the validity of its own deliveries and hold them up to reflective scrutiny. On the best scenario further thought will correct the initial mistake; even on the worst scenario the effort of critical reflection will break up the illusory appearance of conscience as a moral dictator, imposing just one course of action upon us, perhaps the wrong one! The very possibility of moral thinking transforms our experience of the conscience, which is directed to forming judgments, not delivering commands.

Just as Thomas cuts the Gordian knot with the proposal, "one can withdraw from the error," so we may suggest, "one can address the disagreement." Communion should not be broken, but that does not mean disagreement can be ignored. There are ways of addressing serious disagreements that affirm and renew communion by proven willingness and determination to resolve them. And the very attempt to reach a resolution transforms our experience of the disagreement. Disagreements are no more unnegotiable natural forces than deliveries of the mistaken conscience are. They are openings for those who share a common faith to explore and resolve important tensions within the context of communion.

This kind of proposal is, of course, easy to mishear. It can be taken to mean that parties to disagreements must be less than wholly convinced of their position, ready to make room for possible accommodation. When really serious issues are at stake and talk of a *status stantis aut cadentis ecclesiae* begins to rumble like thunder, urging the search for resolution can seem like an invitation to capitulate, to concede essential points before beginning. It can seem as though Scripture is deemed to be inconclusive and ambiguous, so that either side is free to concede the possible right of the other's interpretation. It can seem as though what is needed is an indefinite irresolution about everything important, in which there is no need for, and no possibility of, a decisive closure. But that is all a trick of the light. None of this is implied in the search for agreement. The only thing I concede in committing myself to such a process is that if I could discuss the matter through with an opponent sincerely committed to the church's authorities, Scripture chief among them, the Holy Spirit would open up perspectives that are not immediately apparent, and that patient and scrupulous pursuit of these could lead at least to giving the problem a different shape—a shape I presume will be compatible with, though not precisely identical to, the views I now hold, but which may also be compatible with some of the views my opponent now holds, even if I cannot yet see how. I do not have to think I may be mistaken about the cardinal points of which I am convinced. The only thing I have to think—and this, surely, is not difficult on such a subject!—is that there are things still to be learned by one who is determined to be taught by Scripture how to read the age in which we live.

Every approach to resolving disagreements may turn out to fail. In the end God may have so hardened our hearts that we can see no way through our difficulties and simply find ourselves apart. God may in his judgment scatter a church that lacked the common will to search for its unity in the truth of the gospel. And then there may come a point at which this situation has to be given some kind of institutional expression. Nothing can exclude a priori the worst possibility that certain persons or groups, or even whole churches, may be declared to have left the communion of Jesus Christ. But it must be a declaration, a formal statement of what has obviously come to pass. It cannot be an act to produce a result. The problem with the notion of separation is its expressive, self-purifying character. It will not wait for God to purify his own church in his own time.

Schisms may come, but woe to that church through whom they come! There is no right, or duty, of schism. As unity is given to the church as a gift, so it is taken away as a judgment. But on no account can disunity be a course of action that the church may embrace in pursuit of its mission or identity. The only justified breach is the one we have taken every possible step to avert, the one that lies on the far side of every conciliar process that can be devised.

3 ETHICS *and* AGREEMENT

Can two walk together unless they are agreed?

(Amos 3:3)

THE CREED-MAKING labours of the churches of the fourth and fifth centuries left a series of statements to measure orthodox Christian belief, but no authoritative moral concepts or norms. For the classic liberal theology of the nineteenth and early twentieth centuries this feature of its legacy was disturbing. The concerns of the first-century Council of Jerusalem, the concerns, indeed, of Jesus's own teaching, spoke loudly enough, it seemed, for the priority of ethics. The kingdom of heaven lay not in the iota of difference between *homoousios* and *homoiousios*, but in righteousness and peace and joy. The best that could be said for the creeds, perhaps, was that moral definitions might prove intrusive. The principles of behavior pleasing to God were perfectly well known, to unbelievers as well as believers, but the circumstances of each age required fresh applications of them not to be hampered by decisions of past ages.

Recent mutations in the liberal tradition have effected a re-positioning. We now hear it urged that the grounds of Christian communion are simply creedal, not moral at all. A universal morality, once the solid rock on which the liberal critique of theology was built, has been swallowed up in the shifting sands of change; moral differences can, and should, be accommodated.[1] This is a fairly radical shift of view, and it might seem that the only thing to connect the new liberal pluralism and the universalism it replaced is that they both challenge a reigning ecumenical consensus. The consensus holds that doctrines and moral practices are deeply intertwined, and to agree on the one is to agree on the other.[2] Communion is itself both a moral practice and the *idiōma* of the third person of the Trinity. It would be hard to imagine a morally pluralist Christianity that had not lopped off the Third Article of the creed—which would mean lopping off the church, that common life in the harmony of God's will which is better than toleration. Civil societies are necessarily tolerant to a degree, and intolerant to a degree; they punish what they cannot afford to tolerate, tolerate what they cannot afford to punish. But the communion of the Spirit is harmony; and a church that understands its identity embraces the gift and task of moral agreement from the start. The very concept of *belief*, moreover, involves moral commitment. "Fully to grasp Christ's teachings and to relish them takes an effort to

1. For this point of view, see M. Adams, "Faithfulness in Conflict," 70ff.

2. Cf. Breidenthal, "Disagreement as Communion," 190: "communion names our willingness to embrace unity within the household of faith . . . not so much a formal relationship as a moral practice."

conform the whole of life to him," as Thomas à Kempis says.[3]
Belief is never neutral in respect of practice; the Epistle of James
declared that faith without works is dead. With whatever lati-
tude or rigor, a Christian communion must surely have *some*
idea of its specific moral shape: *these* works are of a kind that
attests living faith, *those* indicate that faith is dead.

The two liberal poles seem to oscillate on either side of
this ecumenical consensus, the one insisting that morality is
primary and universal, reaching even beyond the community
of belief, the other that it is plastic and diverse, even within the
community of belief. But they have more in common than at
first appears. Both maintain a distance between moral and doctrinal belief; both insist that ethical judgments are subject to a
certain variability. In each of these two respects, it would seem
to me, they have a measure of right on their side. But so does
the ecumenical consensus. To reconcile them effectively, to secure the ecumenical consensus and to restore the lost strengths
of liberalism, we need some further clarity on the underlying
issues: the relation of ethics to doctrine, and the kinds of difference that can be sustained within an underlying agreement.

This demands a short digression into the formal charac-
teristics of ethics. And here is a call for patience. But it will have
its reward at last.

"Ethics" is not the name of a descriptive science, like
"chemistry" or "sociology." There is no slice of reality in which
it specializes. Ethics is the explication of the logic of practical
reason that directs our conduct, individual and collective. It
terminates not in a descriptive judgment about how the world
lies, or a slice of the world, but in a practical judgment on how

3. Thomas á Kempis *De imitatione Christi* 1.1.2, echoing John 7:7:
"Qui vult plene et sapide verba Christi intelligere, oportet ut totam vi-
tam suam illi studeat conformare."

we shall conduct ourselves. But since any practical judgment belongs to the same "here and now" as the thinker does, its conclusions may differ from one day to the next, even though the train of reasoning is essentially the same. The historian who told us on Tuesday that the Battle of Hastings took place in 1066 is expected to say the same on Wednesday, barring any new evidence that has come to light in the intervening hours. But the *same* train of practical reasoning by which on Tuesday I decide to post a letter may lead me on Wednesday to pay a personal visit rather than post another one. This implies no revision of my thinking; it is simply that the successive situations require their own decisions.

But that does not mean that the practical reason by which we direct our conduct is *independent* of description. St. Thomas Aquinas spoke of practical reason having its own independent starting-points, its own "axioms"; but that is a misleading picture. Practical reason is more like an *extension* of descriptive reason, going beyond telling how the world lies to judging how we may find our way through it. It builds on descriptive judgments, and if the descriptions it builds on are false, its judgments will be misconceived. The fool who says in his heart "there is no God" will be corrupt and do abominable deeds (Ps 14:1). That is why practical disagreements may sometimes be very perilous. Not all differences of practical judgment can be accounted for in terms of different situations.

Here are three formal coordinates for mapping differences of practical judgment, followed by a brief commentary on each:

1. Some differences of practical judgment are not *ethical* differences, others are.

2. Some ethical differences of judgment do not indicate *underlying moral* disagreements, others do.

3. Some ethical disagreements do not reflect *doctrinal* disagreements, others do.

1. Practical judgments differ *concretely*, simply as distinct events in history. Different judgments are made in different situations by different actors simply because the same river never flows under the same bridge twice. In one sense, then, *any* two moral judgments *must* differ. But that level of difference is quite banal and does not constitute an ethical difference. By "ethical difference" we mean that two judgments have features that can be *contrasted*. This can only occur when they can be classified in kinds. Our deeds fall into *moral* kinds: there are honest deeds and dishonest deeds, resolute deeds and hesitant deeds, impetuous deeds and long-considered deeds. They also fall into *material* kinds: some deeds concern financial transactions, some faithfulness in love, some the telling truth or falsehood, and so on. An ethical difference arises when two deeds alike in material kind differ in moral kind. Deeds of different material kinds are not contrasted ethically. If Renate gets married to her boyfriend this Saturday afternoon while Michelle is busy filling out her tax return, we can draw no conclusions about a difference in moral outlook between Renate and Michelle. There is a variety of things people properly set out to do, and the fact that different people are pursuing different projects at any given time does not imply that there are ethical differences among the agents or their acts. But if Sven and Kostas both their submit their tax returns, and Sven's is truthful while Kostas's is untruthful, then, though everything else about the two acts may be different—different place, different laws, different time, different circumstances, different sums of money

involved—we are also forced to recognise a difference which we can only think of as an ethical difference.

Of course, an apparent difference of this kind may, on further inspection, melt away. Two contrasting decisions may be like one another in material kind, but have different specific features that make, as we say, "all" the difference. In 1939, when both Greece and Denmark faced invasion from fascist powers, Greece, believing it had a trained army, defensible borders and reliable allies, offered forcible resistance; Denmark, knowing that it lacked all these things, capitulated. We may at first assume that the Greek decision was courageous, the Danish uncourageous, or perhaps that the Danish decision was prudent, the Greek imprudent. Yet we will probably be right to hesitate over these judgments, since the question the two nations faced was the same question *only in general terms*. Their differing answers were explained, and perhaps entirely justified, by the specific differences between their situations. We can quite reasonably think that each acted courageously, and each prudently, "in the circumstances."

2. An ethical difference is one that can be expressed in binary terms as contradictory answers to the same practical question. In practical decisions there comes a point at which the multitude of options is reduced to two. The twenty-five possible houses we found on the estate agents' websites are reduced by patient elimination and we have settled on our favorite; what it comes to now is whether we go ahead and offer for it, Yes, or No? And we can test for ethical difference by looking for the question to which two opposite answers are given. (It is possible to exaggerate the importance of this binary moment, of course, just as it is possible to exaggerate the moment of decision in moral behavior as a whole. I offer it only as a formal test to distinguish real from imaginary ethical differences.)

Sven submits a truthful tax return, Kostas an untruthful one. The answers they have given to the same question are opposed like negative and positive values of the one integer. But does that mean they *disagree* about something? If Sven is simply acting morally and Kostas immorally, what are they disagreeing *about*? Only whether to be moral or immoral. On what the moral course really is, they may be entirely agreed. The binary difference seems to mean no more than the presence or absence of active moral responsibility. But *lack* of responsibility is not a *kind* of responsibility. What is not there doesn't count. (Remember the logical parable of the three cats on the mat: the ginger cat, the tabby cat, and the imaginary cat?) We should certainly not think that whenever someone acts immorally he or she must have an alternative set of moral beliefs to account for it. Sin lacks the dignity of a point of view. Only if Kostas has a different way of understanding his situation can we trace his difference with Sven back to a *disagreement*. He may, perhaps, believe that government documents do not require strict veracity; he may believe that tax laws are an unjust imposition; he may believe that his duty to his family is higher than his duty as a citizen. It doesn't matter whether he is right; the point is, there must be *something he believes*, justified or unjustified, if he is to have a disagreement with Sven. A disagreement has more propositional content than a difference of judgment; it is a clash of reasonings, which arises from a difference in describing the way the world lies.

"Ethical disagreement," then, does not mean the same as "sin." Indeed, if we think of sin as sheer willful disobedience, there can be no overlap at all between sin and disagreement; the very fact that someone has reasons for a contrary judgment means she or he is not willfully disobedient. But this voluntarist definition of sin is too narrow. There are culpable faults of thought, too, misunderstandings for which we are to blame. Some moral disagreements—perhaps most of them—are a matter for some blame in some quarter. Yet there is such a thing, as moral theology has long known, as "invincible ignorance."

3. Ethical disagreement may be talked about, then, when two conditions are met: *(a)* opposite practical judgments about what to do, deriving from *(b)* differing descriptive judgments about the way the world lies. But descriptive differences are also of various kinds. There are differing judgments of fact; there are differing judgments of circumstances; there are differing estimations of consequences. A special kind of disagreement arises when there are differing views, or interpretations, of some fundamental truth about the world, a "doctrinal" difference in the theological sense. And these are the disagreements which raise the most painful questions about our unity in the faith of Christ. One church may think that the colonial period of Africa's history was a disgrace to the European churches, another may think it was an honorable phase of Christian mission. Such a difference, however large its practical implications, may be tolerated with charity and good will. But if one church affirms that God created the material world, another that it was made by Satan, that will produce something worse than a major difference of practical judgment; it will constitute a disagreement that can hardly be sustained within Christianity.

And this raises the question of what is meant when it is said that a moral disagreement, such as that over homosexuality, is too small, too unimportant, for the churches to divide over. In the face of potential schism in the Anglican Communion, it invites immediate sympathy to ask, in bewilderment, how such a destructive outcome could derive from such a trivial cause.[4]

There is more than one way in which the concepts "small" and "large" may be applied in this context. In the casuistic moral-theological tradition it used to be said that moral offences might be discounted when they concerned "small" as opposed to "grave matter." If one unwittingly pocketed a large sum of money not one's own, one was obliged to make every effort to restore it; if one unwittingly pocketed a penny, one could cheerfully congratulate oneself on one's good luck. If one *deliberately* stole a penny, of course, an act of contrition was required, for theft is theft; yet even so, returning the penny might not necessarily be the highest priority among one's duties. "Scrupulosity," preoccupation with small matters, was thus recognized as a vice in itself.

Some points of moral disagreement among the churches may be settled by an appeal to "small matter." Suppose that in a Roman Catholic parish in Northern Ireland a well-known republican gangster regularly receives communion from an obviously complicit parish priest—what an irritant to the Protestant neighbors! What an embarrassment to the bishop! Yet the Catholic bishops have made their position quite clear. It is a single case, and an irregular one. So it may be "small matter" in the context of ecumenical relations, and everyone would be wise not to make a *cause célèbre* of it. But this illustration does nothing to illuminate our kind of problem. Nobody argues that the fuss over the New Hampshire consecration was overdone because, after all, it was only *one* gay bishop! The whole point was, a precedent was set, and was intended to be set.

4. For this reaction, see Christopher Lewis's contribution to *Gays and the Future of Anglicanism*, entitled "On Unimportance."

Much more potentially fruitful is the paradigm of "heavy" and "light laws" propounded by the rabbis to arrange the laws of the Pentateuch in some kind of moral ranking-order. In the New Testament we find Jesus himself taking up the rabbinic distinction between "heavy" and "light" commands of the law: the tithing of mint and dill and cumin is less important than justice, mercy, and faith; the supreme command is love of God and neighbor. Before we embrace this model with too much enthusiasm, however, we have to answer a difficult question about how it is to be applied. Once we have said that the law of love is architectonic and that ritual is secondary, how much more does the New Testament tell us about differences of gravity? Do our assumptions about the ranking-order of moral principles correspond to anything in the Scriptures, or are they imported from the common intuitions of our own time? Christians in any period of history, whatever their disagreements, seem to agree with one another on morality more than they agree with Christians of other ages on morality and more than they agree with one another on doctrine. Doctrinal preoccupations tend to be diachronic, linking past communities with present, while moral preoccupations are synchronic, characteristic of their day. The moral profile of Christians today is pretty recognizable across most varieties of church and churchmanship. They believe in international aid and fair trade; they believe in care for AIDS victims; they do not believe in racial discrimination; they believe in families; they tend to think the more abstract forms of capitalist financing morally perilous; they regard making money out of sex as debased, and so on. They have their major disagreements, it goes without saying, and perhaps these appear more ominous against the striking uniformity of their background. But this very uniformity marks contemporary Christians off from Victorian Christians, from early-modern or medieval Christians, and from the Christians of the New Testament era. If we ask why there should be such historical differences, the answer is simple: the priorities we hold are the result of shared judgments about the demands of the age in which we live and act. That is as true for us in our time as it was for the New Testament writers in theirs.

If this observation seems to support a strong historical relativism in regard to ethics, let us correct the impression by stressing its limits. It has to do with the issues we *prioritize*. It does not mean that the church in each age conducts its moral thinking in isolation from the traditions it has received, learning nothing from them and acknowledging no authority. It does not mean that there are no moral lessons to be learned from the New Testament. It does not mean that the only lessons to be learned from the New Testament are highly general moral categories ("justice, mercy, faith"), and that all its more detailed discussions may be set aside. The New Testament can and should exercise authority over our moral thought at both general and specific levels. Yet there remains a work of moral judgment that is properly relative to agents and situations, and this is what shapes the priorities that prevail in given periods. That is why it is more difficult for us to sympathize with the moral attitudes of earlier Christian generations than it is to share their doctrinal convictions; for with our contemporaries we share a common world with its urgent questions and moral challenges. The logic of human historicity is that living in a given age means having a distinct set of practical questions to answer, neither wholly unlike those that faced other generations nor mere repetitions of them. It is to be neither superior to nor independent of the past; but it is to be answerable for our own space and time and for its peculiar possibilities of vice and virtue.

Where does this leave the proposal about the light and the heavy? In the awkward position of a *petitio principi*. In warning us not to make light matters into communion-breaking disagreements, it trades on common priorities that we all assume, and offers the good, if undramatic, advice that we ought not to let ourselves be deflected from priorities we agree on. But what when we disagree? If disagreements did not arise, there would be no reflective way for Christians to respond to changing demands. They would just go on stressing what they had always agreed to be most important thing, and would take no notice of how new challenges were shaping up. So when some Christians see a more ominous threat in a new development than others do, the advice to concentrate on the most important things is no advice at all.

The problem with the proposal to solve this disagreement by dismissing the matter as "light," not "heavy," is that it has latched on to the rabbinic rather than the Christian version of the hierarchy of values. I do not say this to disparage the achievement of the rabbis. Their discovery of the difference between the light and the heavy was a great discovery, and without it Jesus's development of the theme would have been inconceivable. Nevertheless, Jesus and the early Christians did develop it, and they did carry forward the proposition of some rabbis that the highest law was not merely the weightiest of the laws, but in some sense *enveloped and contained* all the others. That is to say: the hierarchy of moral principles was not merely a matter of preferring A to B. The law of God had an organic logic, in which the varied and diverse subject-matter of the laws was brought under the hermeneutic control of a unifying and regulative demand, the law of love.

What follows from this is that the moral weight of any area of moral concern—let us say, the scope of any one of the commandments—will be relative to the way in which its demand interacts with the others and concentrates the regulative command of love upon a particular constellation of historical events and circumstances. The specific moral commands do not present sequestered and self-contained demands. They are different matrices for *one* demand, distributing the way it encounters us within the complex order of the created world. The essential task we face in relation to our own differences of moral judgment is to map those differences carefully, to establish their true dimensions. We face a task of moral description, in which we shall need to call upon all the categories of moral judgment offered us, in the Ten Commands and elsewhere, for a variety of relations and interactions in the service of love.

So we see how inadequate it is to exclaim, "But the issue is not such a very great matter, after all!" There are, indeed, smaller and larger differences; but—and the point is crucial—their size is not determined by the *matter* of the difference as such, but by the *relation* in which it stands to wider agreements and disagreements. The point at issue—whether homosexuality, capitalism, colonial slavery, or something else—is never the whole of what is at stake. Nobody has to make a decision about that and that alone. It would be nice to purify the question to the point when it was about one thing and one thing only; but if we had done that, it would already be nine tenths solved. The question is always, *what does it mean, in this constellation of circumstances, to approve or disapprove of this or that line of* conduct? What relations are present to us in and through it? How do the various refractions of the demand of love within the moral law come together to form an understanding of where we stand? So what looks "small" at first glance can become the subject of the day, the focus of everyone's attention, the test of where each and every person is morally situated, the divide between old friendships and new ones. From outside the historical context it may be hard indeed to comprehend why; but it is part and parcel of historical understanding that we should recognize how one issue acts as a conduit for others. The struggle in the fourth century can appear to be about an iota, but it seemed to those engaged in it to be a struggle over false gods. If we cannot see how that was so, it does not mean that it was not so. It simply means we have not entered into the intellectual dynamics of the time and seen how the largest of alternatives was shaping up for the church. Large alternatives always present themselves in petty choices.

And it is no different with our own age. Understanding the times we live in can be especially difficult. Our initial familiarity with them may be a positive hindrance; it is hard to gain perspective. We must first of all, therefore, take *seriously* the fact that homosexuality has become a dividing issue among us. There is no point in expressing scornful wonder. It is part of the shape of the history we have been given to live through—no more rational and no more irrational than any other history. We must cope with the history we have been thrown into, and reach such understanding of it as we can. To do this, we must ask what great issues this apparently "little" issue mediates, how what is fought over can have become the question of strange gods. But if we press forward resolutely along that path, we may begin to untangle the knot of associations, identify the strange gods, flush them out of their cultural hiding places and leave the question of homosexuality disenchanted of them, ready to be seen precisely for what it is and not as the bearer of some wider cultural decision. That cheerful rationalist Joseph Butler thought that "every thing is what it is, and not another thing."[5]

5. Butler, *Sermons*, preface §33

It would be truer to say that everything is something other than what it is, everything is charged with borrowed significations, alien references to things contiguous. A patient work of interpretation is needed. To try to handle the question peremptorily is to deny what it is we face, which is the culturally shaping force of systems of reference. And to deny that is to refuse the ancient challenge, "Know thyself!"

We return to the question from which we began: what room is there for a "pluralism" in the church's moral beliefs and practices, i.e., the acceptance of tolerable but ethically significant difference? Such an acceptance will not be possible, we must assume, when moral difference reflects significant doctrinal disagreement, bringing the common Christian faith into question. With this negative in place, can we now identify a positive possibility for moral pluralism?

As a definitional baseline, we may say that to recommend moral pluralism is to find not just moral difference but moral *disagreement* respectable. Until the final perfection of the church there will always be moral difference in that there will always be sin as well as righteousness. But what there need not always be is disagreement about whether a given practice counts as sin or righteousness. And pluralism aims to find such disagreement *respectable*, not merely to license it. In a civil political order some moral disagreements are licensed without being commended. When the state permits people to sex-select their children or plunge themselves hopelessly into debt by addictive gambling, it does not necessarily approve of these actions. (Whether we approve of the state's permitting them is a separate question.) We may accept people's freedom to follow such courses, and yet disapprove wholeheartedly. We may think that gambling-addiction should lie beyond the reach of the criminal law, and yet not hesitate to suggest to any addict with whom we have a pastoral relation that his addiction is bad for him and for all connected with him. But to advocate pluralism, we must paradoxically maintain a kind of *approval* of moral judgments of which we disapprove. On the one hand, it is not merely a question of recognizing that in different situations different judgments will be appropriate; for in that case there is no disagreement. To advocate moral pluralism is to say that something which should in principle not be done, should continue to be done all the same. And to advocate it plausibly is harder than may at first appear.

Let us take a paradigm case. Western liberals are inclined to view arranged marriage with disfavor. That young adults should be wholly responsible for finding and choosing their own marriage partners is, they are likely to think, undoubtedly better. There is always a risk of immature judgment, of course; yet the fact that the individuals take responsibility for their own decision at this critical juncture in their lives is morally fitting to their personal dignity, and offers a better prospect that a couple will be committed to each other over the long term. What space does this leave for Western liberals to speak in favor of the more ancient system? They can admit that it fits other expectations within societies that traditionally practice it—e.g., in respect of education, breadth of social contact, the role of affine-groups in providing cultural and economic opportunities, and so on. They can admit that when operated conscientiously it may serve the best interests of young couples *as they actually find themselves situated* in those societies. They can see that reform could not be achieved on this one point without renegotiating a whole range of other social conditions, so that a sudden breach in the tradition could be very difficult to handle; considerate and consultative ways of operating the system, on the other hand, might produce a slow and healthy evolution towards freedom. The Western liberal can grant all this without doubting that the modern Western policy is superior. On these terms Western liberals can be genuine moral pluralists in respect of the question.

This example draws our attention to a necessary condition for any appeal to pluralism. It can be made only on behalf of practices embedded in cultural contexts, contexts in which they serve to secure recognizable social goods. Pluralism, in effect, can only be made sense of in relation to cultural totalities, modes of social existence taken in their entirety. There is a range of different possible patterns for negotiating the challenges of human social existence as a whole. We by no means have to maintain our neutrality in respect of the various features of these; yet we may still recognize that the troubling features play a structural role within their systems. But this has an implication of major importance: the appeal to cultural pluralism can never support experimentation or innovation. It demands deference for established traditional differences, those related to broad patterns of social organization.

Imagine a Western visitor in a society where arranged marriage prevails asking a young woman why she permits her parents to choose a husband for her. If she is articulate, she may rehearse the virtues of the practice in relation to the society she belongs to: "I only know dull uneducated village boys, but my father has contacts with educated families in the city," and so on. If she is reflective, she may also concede the virtues of a system of free choice. And yet, "it is the way it is done here." Pluralism means accepting the validity of this last move, acknowledging a certain authority to embedded practice. But no innovation can be defended in that way; and it is curiously absent-minded of us if we don't find it odd when the defense appropriate to established practices is offered on behalf of innovations or experiments whose likely long-term effects are quite unknown.

Societies may, of course, sometimes be asked to engage in experimental change. But this requires reasons, and the reasons must be strong enough to bear the burden of proof. If the arguments offered are insufficient, the case for innovation is not made, and there is no question of the innovation's commanding respect. If, on the other hand, the burden of proof is met, its success consists precisely in undermining respect for a faltering practice. The most that can then be offered defenders of the *status quo* is the respect and forgiveness due to those who are wrong in good faith. But that is not pluralism either. Which is why I say that pluralism is difficult to argue for successfully. A plea for variety of moral practice very easily turns into an undermining of existing practice. Apart from culturally embedded practices, moral plurality quickly becomes self-contradictory, an assertion of p and $\sim p$ at the same time—or perhaps a delaying tactic while one clears one's throat and gets ready to swallow![6]

To assert the right of plural moral judgment requires a careful account of the systemic social differences that make that right intelligible. So explanation of difference is the essence of a policy of mutual forbearance. It risks adding insult to injury to demand forbearance while at the same time refusing ex-

6. And Professor Adams does not in fact succeed in carrying through her pluralist intentions with any consistency. She concludes her advocacy of live-and-let-live with a rousing call for everyone "to own up to the spiritual violence we have done to gay and lesbian, bisexual and transgendered persons" ("Faithfulness in Crisis," 78). The Church of Nigeria will manage things its own way, to be sure; but the rest of us are to apologize loudly for the Church of Nigeria!

planations. The sharp response to the innovations of Western Anglican churches from the churches of the ex-colonial territories owed much to the fact that the innovating churches had no program of mutual explanation in view. And here, perhaps, the churches of the South and East made a mistake. They attributed the North American uncommunicativeness to racism. It is, on the whole, more likely that the North American churches merely acted, in default of a thorough deliberative process of their own, under the force of strong cultural pressure, the reasons for which they never explained even to themselves, since an ill-conceived doctrine of pluralism persuaded them that thinking was an unnecessary labor. They may have suffered something worse than a bout of racism, if such a thing can be imagined; they may have suffered an implosion of their powers of practical reason, the result of long habits of irresponsibility. And since theology is nothing if not a discipline of common reasoning about God and our life together, unless they recover it, their days of being churches of any kind are numbered.

4 SCRIPTURE and OBEDIENCE

> *O that my ways may be steadfast in keeping your statutes!*
>
> (Ps 119:5)

THE AUTHORS OF the *Windsor Report* thought it was unnecessary and inexact to speak of the authority of Holy Scripture; to speak of the authority of God said everything that needed to be said. And there is an element of truth in this, in that the only authority these books can possibly command is the authority of their role in God's self-announcement; apart from that, they are records of a past culture that may interest us or not, as we choose. Yet we cannot leave it at that. For God's authority authorizes; and it is through authorized persons and activities that we see the effective exercise of God's authority in the world. There is nothing wrong in speaking of the authority of bishops, of councils, of preachers or of the community of the faithful; and at the other end of the spectrum, there is nothing wrong in speaking of the authority of Jesus of

Nazareth. Neither is it inexact, then, to speak of the authority of apostles and prophets, called out by God to write with clarity and sufficiency of the events surrounding Jesus of Nazareth, their context in the history of Israel, and their universal meaning for mankind. These writings are God's chosen means, together with the sacramental acts of the church, of making his self-announcement known to all ages. Scripture is not the first moment of God's self-announcement; that is the historical deeds themselves by which he raised up Israel and Jesus. But neither is it a moment *after* God's self-announcement, a retrospective commentary that could be peeled away, leaving the core intact. Scripture is, we may say, God's administration of his self-announcement, the record he has authorized to it and the seal he has set on it to confirm that it is true.

If we need to say more about the Scriptures than that they are authorized, perhaps we may follow John Webster in speaking of their "sanctification" for their work.[1] That means simply that God has set them apart. As he has set apart a particular race and a particular member of that race for the salvation of the world, so he has set apart particular writers to bear a definite and decisive testimony to what he has done. It was, of course, a *human* testimony they had to bear, a work performed in human ways by human servants. In a thousand ways, the texts that lie between the covers of our Bibles show that they are the product of painstaking and creative human labor and reception. But we must be careful what we make of that word "human." If we glide from speaking of their humanity into implying some kind of inadequacy in them, as though their being human were a shameful secret we have laid bare, a deficiency we are now in a position to patch up, then it is we, not they, that

---

1. Webster, *Holy Scripture*, 17–39.

must stand charged with ignorance and superstition. The humanity of the Scriptures does not entitle us to patronize them. Just as we speak of the sinlessness of the human being Jesus of Nazareth, and some Christians speak of the immaculate human conception of the Virgin Mary, so we may speak quite appropriately of a perfection in Holy Scripture. Its perfection is sui generis, a fitness for its own assigned task. The perfection of the Psalms does not consist in their being the most perfectly metrical verses or containing the most perfect poetic imagery. The perfection of the letters of Paul does not consist in their being the highest examples of epistolary elegance. Neither does the perfection of the historical books consist in their being the most unambiguous records or the most discerning evaluation of sources. The only perfection that counts is this: that God *truly attests himself and his deeds* through this poetry, these letters, this history. The faith required of the reader of Holy Scripture is obedience to the testimony that God bears within them, and that is one and the same as the faith that leads to salvation.

In more ways than one the Christian world now finds itself living "after" the fundamentalist controversy, downstream of those white-water rapids that imperiled theological navigation for a century. There is a widespread sense, for one thing, that the historical exploration of the biblical texts has played itself out, that most of what can be done intelligently on those lines has been done, and that further work is subject to the law of diminishing returns. For another thing, the question of the authority of the biblical texts has been refocused from their historical veridicality to their moral serviceability. This makes a deal of a difference. Those who first raised problems about the Bible's historical veridicality thought they could be confident of its authority in everything that really mattered—i.e., faith and morals, two things that might, to a thoroughgoing liberal, melt into one. To the liberalism that grew out of the skeptical project of historical criticism, the moral authority of the Bible, or at least of the New Testament, was simply self-evident. Moral and religious goodness, it appeared, was either unaffected by the vagaries of history or was in a progressive compact with it. So far have liberal convictions undergone a sea change. Doubts about Scripture's authority today are focused on its competence to guide us through those highly contested moral discernments which have become so common a feature of the late modern world.

But in order to get a view of what authority means in this context, we need a clearer view of what it means to make moral discernments. Certain phantasmic conceptions, which liberals and conservatives often used to hold in common, and which hang around today's discussions like ghosts at the feast, had better be exorcised. Moral truths were conceived of as something like self-evident speculative truths, which, once properly grasped, could hardly be doubted. Christ was to be obeyed because, and to the extent that, his moral teaching self-evidently presented us with those truths to which the moral consciousness bore independent witness. Kant said as much in a famous assertion in the *Groundwork for the Metaphysics of Morals*. That meant that practical moral crises could be viewed only as temptations to the weak in faith, not as real dilemmas to which the answer could be in any doubt. They were challenges to our resolution, to be countered by a more unflinching reassertion of the principles we were taught from the beginning. (Think of the appalling assumptions that generate the melodrama of Scott's *Heart of Midlothian*!) Casuistry, which attempted to resolve dilemmas by making fine distinctions, was dismissed scornfully as a mean abuse of the intellect, designed to produce subtle denials of the obvious. Needless to say, the Bible's wholesale rejection of homosexual conduct was seen, by liberals as well as by conservatives, as entirely of a piece with its moral superiority over pagan cultural values.

But ethics has now fallen out of the realm of the self-evident into the realm of the contested, to which, in truth, it always belonged. And this has made moral consistency look less like a confident conviction of truths evident as the day, more like a faith in truths not seen. It restores to practical reason the atmosphere of insecurity and risk that is native to it. The prayer of the psalmist, "Give me life according to your word!" (Ps 119:107) is the prayer of the faithful reader of Scripture who is ready to take the risk of living by it. This reader does not know everything there is to know about Scripture or about the challenges of life; he does not have the answer to every question; but he is willing to rely on this teaching, to receive it on its own terms, questioning and being questioned by it, in the expectation that God will open up his way before him as he reads, recites, and constantly revisits those testimonies to God's purposes.

If we are inclined to say, as I am, that this is the *authentic* way of understanding obedient practical reason, more suited to the real meaning of discipleship, we should not do so glibly, underestimating the danger. That danger arises in relation to two conjoined intellectual tasks, for neither of which there can be secure rules, two "discernments" that simply have to be made, and may possibly be made wrongly with serious consequences. There is the interpretative task of discerning *what the text means*, on the one hand; and there is the conscientious task of discerning *ourselves and our position as agents in relation to the text*, on the other. The first discernment is *of* the text; the second discernment is *out of* the text. In the first discernment, the text is before us; we read about David, about Peter, about

Jesus, and have to decide what it is that is said about them there. In the second discernment the text is behind us; we do not read about ourselves in the same way that we read about David, Peter and Jesus. Yet it sheds light forward upon us. It provides us with the categories and analogies we need for questioning ourselves and understanding ourselves. The Scripture tells us not to bear false witness against our neighbor. Whether *this* particular ambiguous statement we have it in mind to make will be false, or merely discreet, is something that the Scripture will not tell us; we must judge that for ourselves with the aid of the Holy Spirit. Yet everything the Scripture does tell us about truth and falsehood will contribute to making that judgment possible. The authority of Scripture is proved, then, precisely as it does, in fact, shed light on the decisions we are faced with, forcing us to reevaluate our situation and correct our assumptions about what we are going to do.

Neither of these two discernments is without risk; yet the second is the more highly dangerous. The most mysterious question anyone has to face is not, *what does Scripture mean?* but, *what does the situation I am facing mean?* If we have even begun to appreciate the nature of this question, and how a false judgment of ourselves can lead us to destruction, we shall be on our guard against any hermeneutic proposal to *reverse* the sequence of discernments, starting with our own situation and turning back to Scripture to look for something there to fit it. That presupposes that we already know the answer to the one question we dare not presuppose an answer to. Nevertheless such proposals are common enough in theological discussion, sometimes with a liberal, sometimes with a conservative, slant. It hardly matters which, since the two come closest to each other precisely at the point where they are both furthest from the truth. If the conservative thinks that *all* the scriptural witness to moral behavior can and must be honored somehow, and the liberal that only *some* of it, or only *most* of it, must be honored, what difference does that make if each thinks that conclusion has been reached from some self-evident intuition about what the times require, so that the appeal to the Scripture merely confirms what has already been decided? This is not to take Scripture seriously as an authority. And it is not to take living in the present seriously as a risky business.

For our present purposes, and since much of our discussion so far has been concerned with the current dilemmas of liberal Christianity, let us take up a liberal version of this hermeneutic proposal. We shall have opportunity enough to identify the specifically conservative form of the temptation when we discuss the need for hermeneutic "distance." Help is at hand from a cautiously worded statement of Roman Catholic provenance, representing the proposal at its most modest, and therefore, perhaps, its most seductive. "Here and there," wrote Heinz Schürmann, "among the particular New Testament values and precepts . . . there are time-bound judgments of value and fact, and they show that the Holy Spirit has deepened moral sensitivity through the course of the Church's history and the history of mankind."[2] Bracketing out the mention of time-bound judgments of *fact*, which is irrelevant to our purpose, the important claim here is that some New Testament "judgments of value," being "time-bound," show us how moral sensitivity has "deepened" since they were made. These are, of course, only supposed to be occasional. Sufficient distinctions have been made before this point in the exposition to render most of the New

2. Schürmann, "How Normative," 43. We are told that Schürmann's conception of the relation of Scripture to moral doctrine was "adopted in general terms" by the International Theological Commission in 1974.

Testament amenable to our ethical reasoning without recourse to the "here and there." These occasional "time-bound judgments," then, are an intractable residue, a clinker in the furnace that refuses to burn up. When the author proceeds to urge that a "moral-theological hermeneutics" is in place to handle this recalcitrant material, we know that the word "hermeneutics" cannot bear its customary sense. It does not promise, as might be expected, an *interpretation* of these judgments; it promises only a refusal of them. What is demanded is a clear, though modest, right of repudiation in respect of some "judgments of value," not on the ground that the situation has changed, which could cause no one any difficulty, but simply on the ground that we have made some moral progress since the days when the Holy Spirit spoke through the apostles, and can understand their judgments as immature. It asserts the superior right of our preunderstanding.

It is decisive, of course, that this claim is made in respect of *New Testament* moral judgments. That something will have to be said of the "time-bound character" of some judgments in the *Old* Testament will surprise no one who has learned from the Epistle to the Hebrews to see the pre-Christian vision of the human goal as "fragmentary" and "diverse," looking for an "earthly" rest where the ultimate purpose of God was nothing less than a heavenly sabbath (Heb 1:1, 4:7). To take just one example from that book: the way we think of Joshua's wars of conquest will be affected by our looking for a "heavenly" rest. The conquest narratives will not be taken to afford, directly or indirectly, a moral norm for war making, and that not because of changed situations or perceptions, but simply because their salvation-historical position has been, as it were, overwhelmed by the advent of Christ. But this judgment is based on a Christian reading of history, in which Christ himself fulfils and transforms what has gone before. That is the framework in which the "then" of Joshua is differentiated from the "now" of the Christian epoch. To take the same way with the teachings of the New Testament, on the other hand, would be self-subverting. And to avoid this fall into incoherence, the liberal hermeneutic proposal faces, it would seem to me, a simple alternative. Either it posits some *further* climax of salvation-history over and beyond Christ, some "age of the Spirit" such as Montanus or Joachim conceived of, or a Hegelian dialectical history with an Absolute Future, something, at any rate, that will allow a "deepened moral sensitivity" to which the revelation of the incarnation looks immature and outgrown. Or else it makes a distinction between the normative position of Jesus himself and the subnormative position of the apostolic authors, refusing to claim on their behalf the kind of finality it claims for him. The difficulties into which each of these courses leads are too well known to be pursued in detail at this point.

Since we summoned a Roman Catholic theologian for a modest statement of a hermeneutic proposal that Anglican liberals would be likely to make with less reserve, let us look in the same direction to find a suitable corrective, equally modestly expressed. Jean-Yves Lacoste has written: "The image of the hermeneutic 'circle' is less illuminating than it seems. We can learn only to the extent that we can let the unanticipated put our expectations and our prejudices in question. Authentic discovery punches a hole in the circle, since only pseudo-questions carry their own answers ready and waiting in their bosoms. Pre-understanding without honest admission of non-understanding will hardly invite more than the most meagre discoveries."[3] Lacoste does not challenge the necessity

3. Lacoste, "More Haste, Less Speed," 272.

of hermeneutic preunderstandings. He insists simply that there can be no discovery that has a circular form; preunderstanding cannot have both first and last word. "Yet it is necessary," he continues, "for questions to be asked, and that means there must be a field of dialogue where the speech that answers my questions can become my very own speech."[4] The essential difference between two hermeneutic approaches emerges precisely at this point: the one sees Scripture's readers as armed with "deepened moral sensitivity," new moral confidence that has accrued to the elevated age in which they live and from which the text cannot deflect them, the other sees them as approaching armed with moral *questions* to which they seek answers that may become their "very own." What is at stake in resistance to the liberal hermeneutic paradigm becomes clear: the cause is the cause of *open questions*—questions that need opening and holding open because they are of such importance existentially to those who have to ask them. But to hold a question open with real existential commitment, and not merely to bedazzle the conversation with interrogatives darting round like bats in daylight, one must purposefully look to the source from which an answer is sought, an answer not already contained in the question, which is therefore capable of reforming and refining the question. And that is precisely what is meant by the authority of Scripture in Christian ethics.

Indeed, it is what is meant by the authority of Scripture as such. For authority is what evokes belief and obedience, and questions of belief and obedience are all, at root, moral questions—not in the superficial sense of being related to the details of our behavior, but as concerned with the way we dispose of ourselves in our living. What hermeneutic theory says about

4. Ibid.

preunderstandings applies, of course, to speculative and empirical questions too: the experimental scientist cannot ask questions of the readings he obtains without some preunderstanding of what those readings may indicate; yet he cannot discover anything unless those readings can redetermine his preunderstanding. But we leap into a whole new world of seriousness when the questions are the ultimate practical questions, questions about how we are to live the one life given us; and we leap into a whole new world of seriousness when we dare to ask these questions of God's chosen witnesses, the writers of the documents of the Old and New Testaments.

The liberal hermeneutic paradigm, fashioned by the controversy over historical biblical criticism, failed precisely because it thought it could count on there being a concrete moral truth immediately and categorically known to all, a peremptory and unchallengeable moral certainty. In this it failed to allow for danger. Action is always exposed to danger: we may turn out to have acted on false assumptions about the facts, to have misunderstood the situation in which we acted, to have formed an inadequate conception of our task, to have failed to envisage the good to be pursued, etc., etc. Nothing can guarantee us against such failures; nothing except perpetual vigilance can protect us from them. In failing to allow for danger, the liberal hermeneutic failed to pose the questions that engage us supremely in our self-disposal: questions of intelligibility and purpose in the life we live, questions of our responsibility for ourselves. Always pressing forward in pursuit of some speculative truth, it dared to take the answers to all these questions as read; in doing so, it bypassed deliberative reason and short-circuited the role of the intellect in the living of life.

The questions we pose to Scripture look for answers to help us live as those reborn from death and destruction, exercising our powers of thought and decision anew. We may not look for answers that will excuse us that task. Consider, for example, the question and answer of the psalmist: "How shall a young man keep his way pure? By guarding it in keeping with your word" (Ps 119:9). It is hardly surprising that a long-established line of historical criticism found this profound poem, the most existentially urgent document in the whole Old Testament, to be legalistic, formalistic and altogether uninteresting. That was because the critics never grappled with practical reason as the poet grappled with it. To the poet, presented here as a young man poised on the threshold of life with everything still to be determined, the question mattered. He had need of a word; he had a way to find, and was unsure of it; he wanted it to be not merely *safe* but *pure*—"uncompromised," as we might say, and worthy of a human being's one and only opportunity to live. But why a *word*? Because the only way we have of engaging with our living is by *thinking* about it, and thought requires that we discern a shape, a form, in how we live. An approach to practical reason must be existential, for it is our selves that are at stake in the answers we reach; it must be "poetic" for the task is not mere repetition, but creation in action; but it cannot be improvisatory, since it is a response to a context, and that context may at any point deceive us or trip us up.

To a word of God we turn, then: a word that gives the world its original meaning and intelligibility, and gives our engagement with the world its meaning too. If we fail to envisage the practical question practically, and think of it as merely theoretical, then we shall feel ourselves imposed upon by the claim to authority and shall resist it by outright protest or by calculated dissimulation. Theoretical discussions always look askance at authority, for we can dally over them forever without putting ourselves or other people to the slightest inconvenience. If nobody needs to know whether Jesus was born in Bethlehem of Judea, a text that claims the authority to settle the matter strikes us as intrusive, hemming us in by forbidding speculation that he was born in Waco, Texas. But what if we do need to know? What if it is part of a message about how we may be saved? Then its claim to authority is the very opposite of intrusive; it is a welcome handhold that we may grasp in our struggle for deliverance. And when we come to St. Paul's observation that God has given an idolatrous culture over to homosexuality, or to Jesus's saying that a man who divorces his wife and marries another commits adultery, it is a radical judgment upon human culture and history, a judgment that presupposes the confrontation of God and world. It operates not simply to demand our assent or dissent; it operates to elicit moral decision from us about the kind of life we are to live in faithfulness to its judgment. Its role is to authorize us to live well, not to take authority away from us. So any judgment we make on the authority of that text is, at the same time, a judgment on ourselves, a moment of self-transcendence that it has brought us to achieve.

It sometimes happens, when gays and non-gays meet to explore questions of sexuality, that proceedings will be brought to an embarrassed halt by an impassioned avowal on someone's part of being personally affected: "It is me they are all talking about!" The correct response to such a declaration must be for everyone, of every approach and every point of view, to leap to his or her feet and chime in: "And me!" "And me!" Certainly we had better not approach the famous biblical texts on homosexuality as though we were not personally affected! What business could we possibly have with them if our only interest were to frame a theory of sexuality, or perhaps a history of sexuality, for scientists or philosophers to discuss? We had better come to them knowing that we need the help of God's word if we are to find our way through this idol-ridden sphere, and that our own sexuality and idolatry—nothing less!—are under scrutiny in those texts. The dangerous possibility of moral skepticism had better be always present to our minds, and we had better know the terror of waking up one day to find that the living of our lives has become worthless, in our own sight and in God's. We had better stumble across homosexuality, our own or other people's, as a genuinely unknown quantity; we had better ask about it as those who need to be told, rather than reckon we already know all there is to know. If its opportunities and threats press in on us with bewildering complexity, leaving us at a loss as we search around for a way of sorting out the multiple layers of our experience, then the authority of Scripture may begin to mean something serious to us.

Better an honest bewilderment than a perfect theory. Then, with our preunderstanding up in the air, we shall understand well enough that St. Paul's observations about the relation of homosexual practice to an idolatrous culture are only one moment in the story. Yet we shall be very unwilling to leave that moment out, since we shall be only too conscious of our own predicament with the idolatry of our culture. The danger lies, we shall know, precisely in oversimplification. But oversimplification consists of ruling inconvenient angles out, and we can hardly avoid oversimplification by failing to think about the subtle undercurrents and connections that bind a given sexual dilemma to a given cultural complex. If we cannot approach this text as a clue to a problem weighing sorely upon us (whether as homosexuals ourselves, or as those who share a social space with homosexuals, two categories that include most people in the West), we shall certainly experience it as a pointless imposition. Then we shall rebound in panic, assert the right of our preunderstanding, and briskly close down every question. Protective of a freedom that will, in the end, be no more than purely notional, we shall put ourselves on guard against any insight in any text that might actually teach us something helpful. If only we understood what freedom really meant, and how difficult freedom is to accomplish, we would surely ask that text to give us rivers of living water!

5 HERMENEUTIC DISTANCE

Therefore we must pay greater attention to what we have heard, so that we do not drift away from it.

(Hebrews 2:1)

A DISCIPLINE OF biblical "hermeneutics," i.e., of interpretation, has no point unless we are resolved to be obedient. That will serve as a summary of the argument of the fourth of these "sermons"—and if it seems to leave a number of loose ends hanging, let them hang a bit longer while we press on to the other side of the matter; for without seeing both sides, we cannot get the question of scriptural authority properly in view. The other side is this: obedience is a duty that needs the discipline of hermeneutic reflection if it is to be carried through. We cannot "obey" in a vacuum of understanding.

To get a purchase on the point, let us begin from the case that seems to belie it: what we sometimes call "implicit" obedience. That epithet suggests that there is no room to stop to think. The command is barked out, and the troops leap to it, as in the old sergeant major's quip, "When I say 'jump,' you jump, and ask how high on the way up!" Is this not the right model, after all? Must we not obey God blind, acknowledging that the ways of providence are beyond our grasp? The story of Abraham's sacrifice of Isaac would hardly make sense if there were nothing laudable in simply doing what God commands, questions aside.

Yet even "implicit" obedience demands a measure of understanding. There is an old (and overfamiliar) joke about a man who sought guidance by opening the Bible at random; and coming at first attempt on the statement that Judas went and hanged himself, arrived on the second at "Go, and do thou likewise!" It is not a very funny joke; but a joke it is, not a tragedy. What makes it a joke? Jokes are about fools, and the hero of this joke is certainly a ripe fool who did not understand something very elementary about commanding and being commanded. Commands are events that occur within a relationship. They are given *by* somebody *to* somebody at a particular juncture. The order barked out at the new recruits by the sergeant major needs a parade ground for its context. There must be an understood relation between barker and barked-at. Otherwise what is barked can have no reference, and if it has no reference, it cannot be obeyed. Imagine walking quietly down the street and hearing a voice mysteriously borne through the air: "Present arms!" What are you to do? You will probably suppose you have overheard something not intended for your ears, from a nearby military barracks or a film set. Possibly, though, you think it was the voice of an angel sent to warn or command you—but then you will have to give your mind seriously to interpretation. The one thing you cannot do is simply present arms, like recruits on a parade ground. You don't have arms, only an umbrella. They can obey "implicitly," you can't. And they can only obey by virtue of what is understood within their situation: that they are recruits in training, that they are standing on a parade ground, that the loud-voiced man with the red face shouting at them is their sergeant major, and so on. Implicit obedience needs a frame of reference. Even Abraham had to reckon that this was YHWH speaking to him, the same YHWH whose promise had led him out of Mesopotamia to the land his descendants were to occupy, who could bring his purposes to bear in the teeth of seeming contradiction. The point is emphasized by the writer to the Hebrews: "He considered that God was able to raise men even from the dead" (11:19). That "considering" did not *detract* from his implicit obedience. It made it possible.

I knew someone who had a curious experience in the course of her early education when, seated at the back of a classroom next to an unsoundproofed partition, she ended up learning the next-door class's lesson instead of her own. If a child is to obey when the teacher says "get out your poetry books!" she must be able to tell whether it is *her* class that is being spoken to and *her* teacher who is speaking. To obey we need a context, and we need to relate ourself correctly to the context. The fool in the joke does not know how to relate himself to the commands he reads in the Bible. The problem lies not in the commands, but in a failure of practical reason in himself. We may be tempted to call him "literal-minded," but that doesn't quite get to the bottom of the problem. The biblical texts he landed on make perfectly good literal sense when read on their own terms; nothing would be gained by trying to read them figuratively or allegorically. But he is unable to read them on their own terms at all. Preoccupied with finding a reference to himself, he diverts their literal sense from its proper context into his, and so arrives at a conclusion that they could never, literally or otherwise, have intended.

Commands are acts, and acts are performed at certain times and in certain circumstances for certain definite purposes. Divine commands are acts of God. They exert a claim upon their own historical context primarily, on those to whom they are directly addressed. But because any act has a certain intelligibility in its context, and the context of God's acts is his constant will to bless and redeem the world, God's commands may always have implications for other times and circumstances. The Decalogue was not of interest *only* to a barbarous people gathered at the foot of a mountain in Arabia long ago. We, too, in our time and setting, have ways of honoring our father and our mother and of not coveting our neighbor's goods. But in order to judge the bearing of these commands on other times and circumstances, we must observe their place in their historical context first. If we say, "That applies to us, too!" we are *already* engaged in moral reasoning.

Some of the commands in the Bible are so very "bare," so free of wider implications, so wholly defined by their historical situation, that they could never be obeyed more than once, even analogously: "Go into the village opposite you," Jesus told his disciples, "and immediately you will find an ass tied, and a colt with her; untie them and bring them to me" (Matt 21:2). It might be an edifying liturgical innovation if on Palm Sunday a village congregation would walk across the fields to greet its neighbors and be met there with a suitably domesticated beast of burden for the minister to be escorted back on, all waving palms and singing "All Glory, Laud, and Honor"! Not even on the widest construction, however, could this be obedience to the command that Jesus gave his disciples. That command cannot be obeyed now. On the other hand, there are commands whose content can always make some claim upon obedience, however different the circumstances. Consider the passage in the Sermon on the Mount (Matt 5:21–48) where Jesus says, "You have heard that it was said . . . but I say to you. . . . Be reconciled to your brother . . . if your right hand causes you to sin, cut it off. . . . Do not swear. . . . Do not resist one who is evil. . . . Love your enemies." These are not at all like "untie the colt." They claim to direct our action in certain kinds of situation that arise recurrently.

But these again divide into two types: moral rules and public laws. The moral rules in the Sermon on the Mount are concerned with dispositional attitudes—conciliatoriness, self-discipline, restraint, forgiveness, and so on. They are radically and surprisingly expressed, without much interest in whether we will find them easy to obey or not. They have nothing much to say to such dilemmas of practical casuistry as, "What if my brother refuses to be reconciled unless I join him in a solemn oath of undying hatred to our enemy?" Such questions are left, as it were, for later. As a result, these moral rules are capable of directing our conduct in a wide variety of circumstances and producing a very varied style of conformity. By contrast, public laws are designed to be straightforward and easy to keep with a measure of uniformity in execution. We have an outstanding example of a legal code in Deuteronomy 14–23. Shaped, very evidently, out of preexisting legal traditions, it aims to maintain a practical continuity with these while achieving certain dominant reforming aims. It chooses its topics apparently randomly, in the light of questions that have come up and legal rulings that are to hand. It has a lot to say about detailed dilemmas, comparatively little (though not nothing) about underlying attitudes. Moral rules and public laws look different, and they do different jobs. In obvious ways, moral rules are more "portable," more easily applied to changing situations. We still have brothers to be reconciled to, even if there is no temple to leave our gift in (cf. Matt 5:23–24). We would have considerable difficulty in obeying the Deuteronomic law of slavery, however sympathetic we might be to its intentions.

These two types of generic instruction, as they appear in the Bible, share a common feature. They are framed by a narrative context. The metaphor of "framing" could be misleading, though, for a picture frame is designed to display the picture, and may be taken off and changed, but this framework is integral. Narrative is a constituent element in these texts' moral claim upon us. The legal code of Deuteronomy 14–23 is preceded by twelve chapters of mixed narrative and exhortation, explaining how this law code originated in the birth of the nation and the ministry of Moses, and why a code originating in Israel's nomadic past should have authority over an settled agricultural society governed by a monarchy and civic institutions. This setting is continually relevant for understanding the commands as they arise. When told that we must leave the gleanings of the grape harvest for the stranger passing by (Deut 24:19–21), we are reminded that God heard our cry when we were strangers in the land of Egypt (Deut 24:22). The Sermon on the Mount, similarly, is situated in St. Matthew's Gospel as a prelude to Jesus's ministry and as a climax to the account of his birth and commissioning. This, equally, is not irrelevant to those who come to this text for guidance. When we are told to resist not evil, we are prepared to hear how Jesus refused to call on legions of angels to resist arrest in Gethsemane (Matt 26:53–54). The difference in the content of the two texts corresponds to the difference in the narrative that supports them: on the one hand, a narrative about the founding of a holy nation; on the other, a narrative about the fulfillment of history and the redemption of the world. Neither is "timeless," if by that we mean detached from any historical context. But there is a sense in which we can call the Sermon on the Mount "timeless," while Deuteronomy is not. Here is the point at which the particular history of a nation with which God dealt is taken up into God's all-embracing act of world redemption; here is the event in which we are all in every age involved, and here are the commands that belong to that all-embracing event. At the center of the biblical message is an announcement of what God has done in history—"when the time had fully come, God sent forth his Son" (Gal 4:4)—and in that announcement all the authority of the biblical texts finds its source. Biblical commands speak with authority to us because that deed of God in history speaks with authority to us. Let us sum it up like this: it is not *the commands the Bible contains* that we obey; it is *the purposes of God that those commands reveal*, taken in their context. The purposes of God are the ultimate reason why anything at all is good or evil to do. The Bible is authoritative for ethics because it speaks of those purposes and demonstrates them through God's acts in history.

We began from commands because they are a limiting case, raising the question of "implicit" obedience most sharply. There are, of course, other forms of moral instruction in the Scriptures. An ancient and uncouth tradition of hermeneutics looked exclusively to commands as a source for ethics. A fifth-century work called *Speculum 'Quis ignorat?'* wrongly attributed to St. Augustine, begins: "Who does not know that within Holy Scripture there are propositions to be understood and believed, and commands and prohibitions to be observed and acted upon?" and proceeds rather tediously to attempt a list of all the commands in Scripture, so that we may have a compendious code of instruction from which nothing is omitted. It is a model of how not to approach the question, for the effect, of course, is to omit what must on no account be omitted from any view of the Bible's moral instruction: stories, hymns of praise, prophecy, wisdom, parables, lists of virtues, and so on. These all teach us to direct our ways pleasingly to God. We can learn of the wrong of adultery from David and Bathsheba, and not only from the seventh command of the Decalogue. But of all these other styles of moral communication, the same must be said as was said about commands: they lay claim upon our action by virtue of what God has done for us and with us.

Is that to say that everything in the Bible is ethics, and that there is no specifically moral teaching, distinct from history or doctrine? No. There is moral teaching as distinct from doctrine in the same sense that there is practical reason as distinct from theoretical reason. The narrative of how Abraham took his men and chased after the four kings to recover Lot is, viewed in isolation, simply a factual proposition with no term beyond itself. But it does not stand in isolation. It is integrated into the Pentateuch, and the Pentateuch is integrated into Scripture. Our reading of Scripture, viewed as a whole, always tends towards a practical term, how we are to live before the living God of Abraham. There are texts that focus especially upon this practical cutting edge; yet everything in Scripture has a bearing towards it and nothing is simply irrelevant to it. Yet it is not wrong to treat those texts where narrative and doctrine and liturgy crystallize into direct moral instruction as having a special interpretative weight. For these afford a paradigm of how faith works in action, and so serve to protect our moral reflection from falling into a kind of speculative hermeneutical fancy. They are a check on what we are doing with the Bible. If we cannot make our interpretation accommodate the passages where the biblical authors give direct practical guidance, something must have gone wrong. That is why such texts as the condemnations of homosexuality should continue to demand our careful attention, even though they should never be treated alone and in isolation. They are a test of our capacity to achieve a faithful overall reading of the Scriptures. If we can make nothing of them, we should go back to the beginning and start again.

All this takes us a considerable distance from "implicit" obedience, a response that requires no thought or consideration but only immediate conformity. There are occasions on which nothing but implicit obedience will do. But recognizing those occasions depends on a general understanding that we have to think through patiently and reflectively. And when the church is at sea, for one reason or another, over how to read the message of the Gospels, only patient attention to reading, interpretation and obedient thought will bring it to harbor. A shrill call for implicit obedience never substitutes for careful exploration of what it is that must be obeyed.

Is all this just another way of intellectualizing the demand of God? Does it subvert the call for obedience, which ought to be a matter of immediate devotion? To the first of these questions we should answer, Yes—in a way; to the second we may answer, No. Yes, in that our obedience *must be thoughtful obedience.* This "must" is, in the end, not so much an obligation as a simple necessity. Moral instruction is directed to what we "do," and nobody "does" without thinking. If obedience is what is required, thought is what is required—thought about how we may frame our action obediently to the demand. But thoughtful obedience does not exclude immediate encounter with the commanding God. Moments of fear and trembling may befall us; and these are not an *alternative* to the "rational worship" of Romans 12:1–2, by which our minds are renewed to "appreciate distinctions." It is really just another way of saying that the obedience to Scripture that is required of us is the obedience *of faith.*

And in that obedience of faith there has to be a "hermeneutic distance." That term refers to the gap between the reader and the text, the gap that understanding has to bridge. This "distance" is often misunderstood. It is not *historical* distance—that particular turn in hermeneutic theory led, in my view, into a blind alley. There is no reason why I should find the gap wider when reading Plato than when reading Lévinas. Of course, texts that come from unfamiliar cultural backgrounds present special tasks; but if we are ready to take up those tasks and familiarize ourselves with their backgrounds, they need not be any more alien to us in the end. Possibly they will be less so. We may suppose all too carelessly that just because we are contemporary with Lévinas, we shall understand his meaning and objectives without much effort. The distance we have to insist on, rather, is that which secures the objective standing of a text, and especially of a text that claims to speak to us in the name of God. The distance between the text and ourselves can never be, and should never be supposed to be, swallowed up by our understanding. Whatever I may have concluded from my reading of the Scriptures, my conclusion must be open to fresh scrutiny on fresh reading—and will in fact always be, whether I know it or not, because the Scriptures will be its judge. If, after reading the Bible faithfully, I am confident enough to make a ringing declaration of what I have understood, and if my confidence is wholly justified as far as it goes, that still does not mean that my declaration was simply identical to what was contained in the Bible. I may declare that the eternal Word of God, consubstantial and coeternal with the Father, was incarnate of the Virgin Mary; I may be perfectly entitled to think my statement "biblical," as well as "catholic" and "orthodox," and whatever other epithet may underline its authenticity as an expression of Christian belief; and yet it remains the case that those words are not in the Bible, and their authority is always a matter of demonstration and argument in the light of other words that are in the Bible. The authority of Scripture cannot be made over in full plenitude to my words, or to any other words.

There is, of course, a proper authority attaching to a faithful formulation. Creeds, declarations of church councils, Reformation articles and confessions, even the propositions of major theologians have exercised wide authority in the church, and deservedly. Are there moral formulae that have equivalent standing to these doctrinal formulae? Probably. But the drafters of these formulae were not appointed eyewitnesses of the incarnation, as Peter and James and John were eyewitnesses of the incarnation, and so the question whether they have adequately caught the Scriptures' implication at this or that point will always be worth discussing, even if the result of the discussion is the same every time. A seriously meant inquiry into what the Bible means and how it may apply to us can never be out of place in the church. We must not, then, in the supposed defense of a "biblical" ethic, try to close down moral discussions prescriptively, announcing that we already know what the Bible teaches and forbidding further examination. It is the characteristic "conservative" temptation to erect a moment in scriptural interpretation into an unrevisable norm that will substitute, conveniently and less ambiguously, for Scripture itself. The word "authority" means, quite simply, that we have to keep looking back to *this* source if we are to stay on the right track. Anything else is unbelief—a refusal to open ourselves to the question, What is God saying to us through his word?

The three temptations of Jesus, temptations, as St. Luke recounts them, of body, soul, and spirit, culminate on the pinnacle of the temple where the devil invites Jesus to demonstrate his belief in Scripture as God's word. Jesus replies, "You shall not tempt the Lord your God." (Luke 4:12). The fulfillment of the word is sure; but it is not for us—not even for Jesus—to impose on God the manner and time of its fulfillment. At the point of greatest confidence between God and man, where God has shown to man his mind and his purpose, the Son of Man stands back, refuses to seize the initiative and waits upon the unfolding of the Father's purposes that have already begun to unfold. The interpretation of Scripture is a matter in which we wait upon God—not, of course, as though we had understood *nothing* of his mind, but simply because we have not understood *everything*. The text and my reading of the text are two things, not one, and the first is the judge of the second. I can always read further, study harder, think deeper. To precipitate myself from the pinnacle of the text, and demand that angel wings shall bear my interpretation up, is to cut short the task of waiting and attending; it is to tempt the Lord my God.

Why should we find this so difficult to accept? We are anxious for the church. We are anxious for ourselves. We are anxious about the consequences of admitting any indeterminacy in our understanding of the text, which might give a hostage to fortune. Once we acknowledge hermeneutic distance, we fear, "anything goes." A host of false prophets will take advantage of our respectful distance. They will rush forward to wrest Scripture from its plain sense, pervert it into authorizing what cannot be authorized. And, of course, this fear is, in the short run, likely to prove well grounded. The public discourse of theology is, indeed, one where anything has the habit of going. False prophets are, and always will be, quick to rush forward. So we must simply expect to hear abominations and absurdities put forward with implausible but brazen claims to be consistent with, or authorized by, Scripture. To this annoyance we are called, as Christ warned and as generations of the faithful have since proved. The question is, what sacrifice of faith we would make if, to avoid this annoyance for ourselves and to spare the church its turmoils, we were to close down on the reading and interpretation of Holy Scripture, if we were to declare that there was nothing to discuss any more. To our fears, all too well grounded in the short term, we must reply with the question: is the Spirit of the living God an adequate match for human perversity? Is Jesus's promise about the gates of hell meant seriously enough to be relied on? Are we prepared to encounter false interpretations with the weapons of true interpretation, the weapons that are "not worldly, but have divine power to destroy strongholds . . . [taking] every thought captive to obey Christ" (2 Cor 10:4–5)? Precisely those weapons—hand-to-hand, thought-to-thought, unpicking the web of error strand by strand—cannot be used without discourse, without argument and debate, without proper distance on, and attention to, the text in itself, without the waiting and searching that every true work of interpretation demands.

Granted that this is what we are called to, we may ask: Do we, does the gospel, then, have no *formal and institutional* defense against indefinite prevarication and distortion? Indeed we do, and it does. There is within the church the *ministry of the word*, which has the duty of ruling false interpretations out and ruling true interpretations in. That is what our priests and bishops are charged with, and they do it not by suppressing or forbidding the discussion of the biblical witness, but by waiting on the mind of the church where it is genuinely seeking to understand, and by confirming the mind of the church where there are well-established lines of understanding. In a situation of controversy, this ministry will exercise a proper caution and refuse to allow the church to be swept off its feet by sudden enthusiasms, or shamed out of its traditional judgments by the power of new fashions. It will create and hold open the space for properly disciplined and biblically founded common inquiry.

And may it also from time to time pronounce, as Richard Hooker hoped it might, a "judicial and definitive sentence, whereunto neither part that contendeth may under any pretence or colour refuse to stand"?[1] The difficulty is, as Hooker himself was forced to recognize, that if the mind of the church is in fact unsettled and uncertain, declaring that a pronouncement is definitive will not settle it, but will only heighten the tension. In James Joyce's story "Grace," the ideal of a judgment that settles everything is subjected to some teasing, as an enthusiastic Irish layman, aiming to save the soul of a dissolute colleague, gathers with some friends around his bed and renarrates, suitably reinforced by some "special whisky," the history of the ratification of the infallibility dogma at the First Vatican Council:

> "In the sacred college, you know, of cardinals and archbishops and bishops there were two men who held out against it while the others were all for it . . .
>
> "Ha!" said Mr. M'Coy.
>
> "And they were a German cardinal by the name of Dolling . . . or Dowling . . . or –"
>
> "Dowling was no German, and that's a sure five," said Mr. Power, laughing.
>
> "Well, this great German cardinal, whatever his name was, was one; and the other was John MacHale."
>
> "What?" cried Mr. Kernan. "Is it John of Tuam?"

---

1. *Of the Laws of Ecclesiastical Polity,* preface 6.1.

"There they were at it, all the cardinals and bishops and archbishops from all the ends of the earth and these two fighting dog and devil until at last the Pope himself stood up and declared infallibility a dogma of the Church *ex cathedra*. On the very moment John MacHale, who had been arguing and arguing against it, stood up and shouted out with the voice of a lion; "*Credo!*"

"*I believe!*" said Mr. Fogarty.

"*Credo!*" said Mr. Cunningham. "That showed the faith he had. He submitted the moment the Pope spoke."

"And what about Dowling?" asked Mr. M'Coy.

"The German cardinal wouldn't submit. He left the Church."

Mr. Cunningham's words had built up the vast image of the Church in the minds of his hearers.[2]

But precisely that "vast image" of church authority is the problem. The bishops cannot and must not substitute their own pronouncements for a hard-sought unity of the Spirit. Yet that does not mean that the bishops have nothing to contribute. What they may and can do—in support of the search for unity, not in suppression of it—is to secure the *tradition* of interpreting God's word as a critical point of reference, and so defend the identity of the community as grounded in faithfulness to the word of God. In this way they may restrain the tendency to anarchy and strife that naturally attends on excitement and uncertainty; they may give structure and order to the processes of faithful inquiry, by keeping before the church's eyes

2. Joyce, "Grace," 130–31.

a clear sense of what comes first and what comes after, what is legitimately in doubt and what cannot be in doubt. And in this context—not to suppress dissent or preclude discussion, but to give the discussion the direction it needs in the service of the gospel—they may perhaps declare that some aspect of a question that was once open is now closed, or that some other aspect of a question cannot be opened until more fundamental questions have been dealt with. In these conditions, their gift of the Spirit will be shown, by facilitating real convergence, to have served the search for unity in God's will.

The Anglican bishops at Lambeth 1998 sought to exercise this gift—and though, perhaps, they did not exercise it perfectly, they spoke with a degree of coherence that was remarkable considering the reports of procedural mayhem that surrounded the occasion. In "rejecting homosexual practice as incompatible with Scripture," they clearly did not suppose they had achieved a simple closure of all the moral questions; they had simply provided a reference point in Scripture to which all answers to these questions would be responsible. They sought to establish some practical conditions for an orderly exploration. Chief among these, they "could not advise" the blessing of same-sex unions or the ordination of those involved in them. An open exploration could hardly go forward if new facts were deliberately being created on the ground by unilateral action. There was, of course, no leonine roar of *Credo!* from the opposition. That was hardly to be looked for, or even desired. What could have been looked for and desired was some patience and restraint. Those who thought it too much to show *that* degree of deference to the authority of the church's ministry refused something far greater than poor Dr. Döllinger ever did. But the last word has still to be spoken in response, and the effect of the Lambeth bishops' service still to be seen.

Meanwhile here we are with five chapters behind us discussing the questions of the church's order, the influences to which it has been subject, and the authority that it must confess. It is quite enough. In the two that remain, we shall turn our eyes back, and forward, to the content of the interrupted exploration, and to some questions that are certainly at issue in it.

6 CREATION, REDEMPTION, and NATURE

Creation waits with eager longing for the revealing of the children of God.

(Rom 8:19)

WHEN THE GOVERNING committee of the Church of Sweden proposed to its General Synod the sacramental celebration of same-sex marriage, it wrote: "Here the distinction between what belongs to creation and what belongs to salvation loses its significance."[1] Innovative as the sacramental proposal was, it is the doctrinal proposal that is likely to shake the foundations. The creation of the world by God and its redemption in Jesus Christ are the poles in relation to which Christians have consistently narrated the moral history of the world. There are moments in the narration, of course, that do not lie at either pole but in between them—e.g., the sacraments themselves, which have no place either in the Garden of Eden or in the

---

1. Church Board of the Church of Sweden, *Life Together*.

New Jerusalem. But these still depend on the *distinction* of creation and redemption; they are sustained by the dynamic tension between them. If the distinction between creation and redemption has no significance, then a sacrament has no significance either. The narrative of creation and redemption has accompanied and disciplined Christian attempts to think about the moral dilemmas thrown up by every age: slavery, war, technology, wealth and markets, etc., etc. In each dilemma, they have asked, what gifts of the Creator are to be rejoiced in here? What evils are to be repented of and lamented? What transformations are yet to be hoped for? As these strands in each dilemma have been separated and clarified, so resolution has seemed possible. But now, it is suggested, the same-sex question is better thought about without this narration. In contemplating a same-sex union we need not ask whether we are rejoicing in the bounty of creation, lamenting the distortion of human affections, or looking forward to the lineaments of the new creation. What could such a proposal amount to—in relation to this or to any other question?

When people ask with greater or lesser bewilderment why *this* issue should have proved so divisive in the churches of our time, one answer lies close to hand: it is anxiety about doctrinal revisionism. The origins of this anxiety lie more than a century back, in the growth of critical academic theology, that speculative anthill from which so many questions have marched forth to nibble at the Christianity of the Scriptures and the creeds. But the focus of anxiety now is not now upon university departments, where reconstructing Christianity from the ground up is out of fashion, but upon diocesan offices and synods. Yet if this is the true meaning of the crisis over homosexuality, it remains to be seen *whose* meaning it is. Is doctrinal revisionism a frontier reached by gay Christians in pursuit of their moral challenge to the church? Or is the gay movement a frontier reached by a liberal church leadership in its pursuit of a doctrinal-revisionist agenda? It was because the answer to this question did not seem at all obvious, that the authors of the "St. Andrew's Day Statement" ten years ago framed their contribution in the form of a doctrinal confession, and asked gay Christians to say how far they could go along with it. Nobody can speak for gay Christians about doctrine except gay Christians, and until an intellectual gay voice is as widely heard in the Christian community as it has long been outside it, there is little point in anyone asserting what gays do or do not believe in. There have been straws in the wind, however, suggesting that not all gays are enamored of the liberal bear-hug.

The dialectic of creation and redemption is not merely one episode in the struggle between orthodoxy and revision. It is its central and decisive battleground. It gives their shape to the creeds that differentiate Christianity from deism. What is it, then, that tempts Christians to loosen their hold on it? What is the underlying doubt that causes them, with greater or lesser embarrassment, to shuffle uncertainly towards doctrinal revision at this decisive point? The answer is, as I take it, a simple moral mistake, centrally characteristic of liberal Christianity. The mistake is called "historicism," and it consists in confusing the good with the future. It induces a profound loss of nerve over any claim to discern the good hand of God within the order of a good creation.

I want to explore this answer more deeply with the help of a recent essay by Professor R. M. Adams, a Christian philosopher with a well-earned reputation for having breathed new life into moral philosophy by recovering the central importance of the notion of the good.[2] Adams's short contribution to the pro-gay cause is an essay in three parts, of which the first sets out a critical challenge to the objection that homosexuality is "unnatural." He makes a deft job, as one would expect, of marshalling some of the more common objections to the use of "nature" as a normative category: it depends on an Aristotelian conception of species; laws of nature are merely statistical; a species is simply a population of similar genetic traits; the use of "natural" and "unnatural" to express moral discrimination is untheoretical, supplying no reason for favoring or disfavoring anything. Natural teleology is of interest today, Adams holds, only to some Roman Catholics. (That it was the view of Hooker, Taylor, Butler and all the classical Anglican divines, this generous Presbyterian omits to mention, sparing our blushes!) What "most of us" think, Adams holds, granting too much too quickly, I would judge, to the views of Richard Dawkins, is that functional behavior is measured by the successful gene propagation of individual organisms. At any rate, in discriminating between good and evil behavior, as we must, we should not confuse genuine moral intuitions with subjective likes and dislikes. Adams shudders at the thought of eating grasshoppers, though he knows some people like them.

So far the common objections to the objection. Pausing at this point, we may observe that "so far" is not actually *very* far. One might, I think, concede more or less everything Adams says in this section of his essay, and still go on saying that homosexuality was "unnatural." One would have to allow, of course, that the term was derived from a now-outdated Aristotelian notion—one would be mistaken, but one would have to allow it!—yet that need not rule out a post-Aristotelian correlation

2. Adams, "Human Nature." Adams's major contribution to the philosophy of the good is *Finite and Infinite Goods*.

of kinds and goods. One would have to allow that expressing a moral intuition in this way was untheoretical, needing
a deeper level of justifying description; but for most people
most of the time it is enough to be reasonably sure that such
a deeper description could in principle be given. But of which
moral intuition may that *not* be the case? Express the view that
it would be "unnatural" for a human infant to be brought up by
chimpanzees. Call it "unnatural" for deaf parents to want their
child to be as deaf as they are. Observe that it is an "unnatural"
diet that destroys the human body by clogging up the valves of
the heart with trans-fatty acids or coating the lungs with tar.
Contrast a Caesarean operation with "natural childbirth." All
these uses of "natural" and "unnatural" are subject to the same
line of criticism as calling homosexuality unnatural—and that
does not make all, or any, of these moral intuitions wrong; it
merely means that they require further explication and justification. Adams's argument is addressed simply to the efficiency
and clarity of one element of our moral vocabulary; and from
such an argument as that one can never expect to reach a substantive conclusion that different sexual orientations are of no
more moral importance than differences of taste over eating
grasshoppers.

So we could stand stubbornly by the substance of the
objection that homosexuality is unnatural, while conceding
more or less all these objections to the objection. But I think
it would be injudicious to concede anything like as much as
this. In the first place, consider the bogey of Aristotelianism.
One so deeply versed in seventeenth-century moral thought
as Professor Adams can hardly be unaware that the wide cur-
rency given to the category of "nature" in that period actually
owed less to Aristotle than it did to Stoic influences mediated
through Cicero. As the philosophers of the early Enlightenment

used it, "nature" can be seen to do a fairly precise job, and to do it tolerably well. That job was to focus attention on the dual constitution of the human being as body and soul, at once a free, self-directing, spiritual entity and at the same time a material organism. The virtue of "living according to nature" was precisely that of harmonizing the demands of these two aspects of one's being, achieving a rational self-direction that respected the structural limits and possibilities of the bodily condition. "Natural" and "unnatural" are terms that come into play when questions arise about how we shall conduct ourselves as embodied souls and ensouled bodies.

At the cost of a slight detour from Professor Adams's argument, we should note that there are strong Christian grounds for interest in such a line of questioning. It is commonly said— though the generalization has nothing to recommend it other than the charm of naiveté—that Christianity traditionally despised and ignored the body. The opposite is the truth. Belief in the incarnation made any such attitude impossible. Even in the eighteenth century, when the temptation for enlightened souls to take wing was, perhaps, at its height, Christians would sing:

> Soul! Make no offence of this,
> That the Light of spirits' bliss,
> True likeness of God's radiance,
> Takes disguise of servile stance![3]

Christianity has, in fact, harped upon the body. It has harped upon the conditions of the body's mortal existence, and it has harped upon the body's share in the hope of the kingdom of God. "No one hates his own body," says St. Paul, "but nourishes and cherishes it" (Eph 5:29). And if Christianity

3. From Salomo Franck's libretto for Bach's Cantata BWV 186, *Ärgre dich, o Seele, nicht*; translation mine.

has earned little credit for its harping, that is because its late modern critics have their own ideas of what should be said about the body, which often begins and ends with the body's erotic powers. Talk of the body's sickness or death is all too easily dismissed as talking the body down. *Gute Nacht, o Wesen!* Christians sing to their dying bodies with all due respect and seriousness.[4] But it is not a song the late modern eroticist wants to hum along to!

To "cherish" the body is to care for very much about the body besides its erotic powers. It is to care for its internal organs and their functions, for the extraordinary capacities of its hands and feet, for its processes of growth. It is to take care of its weight, its rhythms of sleeping and waking, its powers of hearing and seeing. Even if we make a sharp distinction between the *created* and the *fallen* body, so bracketing out illness and death, we can hardly attend to the body and cherish it if we fail to notice its temporality, its exposure to physical risk, or its processes of aging. Jean-Yves Lacoste has reminded us recently that the phenomenon of fatigue cannot be assimilated to illness and suffering.[5] Yet sickness and death should not, in fact, be excluded from our view, for Christians have historically seen mortality not as an accident befalling human bodies, but as a created possibility of bodily life that never need have become an actuality. But above all these things, we have to cherish the body's role in interpersonal communications, its essential sociality. It is through the face that one human being is known to another, and all types of relation are built up through the body's strategies of nearness and distance: its attraction and repulsion,

4. Bach again. These words are from the seventeenth-century hymn "Jesu, meine Freude," by Johann Franck, used as the basis of the motet of that name, BWV 227.

5. "Petite phénoménologie de la fatigue," in *Presence et Parousie*.

its power to dominate and threaten, and its power to charm and endear. And this entails the learning of disciplines that surround the body's bearing of itself. We can none of us endure everybody else's bodies intruding constantly on our own; society is enabled by sustaining spaces around bodies, by holding the body back as well as bringing it forward, by turning the eyes away from it as well as fixing our gaze upon it. Gesture, clothing, styles and patterns of movement, all contribute to form the software by which the body loads its repertoire of social arts and achievements.

The *erotic* body, in fact, stands out as the exceptional moment in the repertoire. Here the body conveys a hint of eternity that beckons and calls us from beyond it; here it reaches out to point beyond itself. It was surely an irrevocable insight on Plato's part (whatever reservations we may have about the rest of his theory of love) to see in eros an *implicitly philosophical* reaction to the human body. It is possible, of course, to use the word "erotic," as a great many of our contemporaries do, simply as a synonym for sexual desire. But that is to miss almost everything of interest that has been thought about the erotic. Eros is precisely *not* sexual impulse; it is an aspect of the spiritual life of mankind, though inevitably engendering bodily experiences to accompany it since we are psychosomatic beings whose every moment is a mediation of the spiritual through the bodily. Reflecting on the body, it responds with yearning for its lurking hint of beauty and truth. It responds to something beckoning through it from beyond it. Precisely that moment of reflection is the temptation, as Plato, again, understood. The familiar body, the body that we live in, object of wonder though it is, is too essentially present to us, too intimate, too enclosing—let us say, too *heavy* to beckon us beyond itself. But the body of the spiritual imagination is light and elusive. If we fail to carry the act of reflection through to its conclusion, if we fail to inquire what the erotic body is a medium *for,* then we end up invest-ing our perfectly ordinary experiences of sexual attraction with an ontological weight that is, in fact, a borrowed transference, and in our confusion we fail to understand either ourselves or our bodies. We cannot and should not take that moment of rapture in the presence of the beautiful body quite at its face value—though we cannot and should not ignore it, either. We must interrogate it for its meaning. So Plato taught, and much Christian philosophy after him; for Christianity mostly (though not universally) found this aspect of Plato's thought suggestive and helpful. His warning has been echoed in most Christian thought about the erotic; it was certainly echoed by Rowan Williams, in his characteristically indirect way, in the much-celebrated but little-understood essay on "The Body's Grace." An unwelcome warning, perhaps, to an ethical intuitionism that puts its trust in the immediacy of feeling; and since Plato, by and large, is more spoken of than read, Christianity has had to shoulder the blame for the reserve—though it never was a reserve *at the body,* but a reserve *at the erotic image* of the body. Ever since St. Paul, it has been the *phronēma sarkos,* "the mind caught on the flesh," not the flesh itself, that has caused alarm.

The "unnatural," then, is a falling short, or perhaps an overreaching, of the transcendence of the soul over the body. Still, Christianity has not been content to leave philosophical programs for transcendence where it found them; and that is because it has had a more complex and more critical view of transcendence than most philosophy has had. There is bad transcendence as well as good. And there is a transcendence *of* the terms of creation as well as a transcendence *within* the terms of creation. Getting a distance on the body is not an end in itself, and may even be a temptation. The key to achieving the *right* distance is to locate the powers of the soul precisely where every created power of human nature must stand, under the judgment of God and awaiting his transforming redemption. The language of "nature" and its concerns for the body-soul relation must be framed within a fully theological account of creation and redemption.

What we have achieved by our digression into the concept of the "natural" is to identify a range of features in human existence that ought to excite our wonder and admiration, and can clearly ground some moral discernments. These then point the way to the understanding that a doctrine of creation can supply. Adams, for his part, having cut short his treatment of the natural with the common objections, finds himself at a loss, when in the second part of his essay he addresses creation, to know what moral discernments this category could possibly disclose. What worries him especially is the difficulty of speaking of a world at the same time created and fallen. If we distinguish a "natural" created world from an "actual" fallen world, he complains, it "breaks the epistemological teeth" of the concept of the natural and unnatural. Is war natural, or merely actual? And how would we know the difference? We can only pretend to do this, he fears, on the basis of "presuppositions" about the purposes or commands of God, which look as though they are smuggled in to make sense of a creation that, on its own, is unable to tell the difference between good and evil. But this is altogether too skeptical. There are some value distinctions we may make quite clearly simply by reflecting upon the way the world works.

Consider, for example, how we know the difference between the health of a natural organism and its sickness—let us say, between the flushed cheek caused by a high temperature and the ruddy glow in the cheek promoted by a vigorous walk.

We could, of course, say that nature knows of no such distinction; that it is only our own preferences that make us call the one flushed cheek "health" and the other "sickness." But the preferences are obviously not arbitrary; they have to do with the predictable outcomes of high fevers on the one hand and of good circulation on the other, with the subjective experiences we have of the one and the other, and with our innate resistance to the prospect of dying. This is all "nature," too. Nature is, to be sure, highly dialectical. She assigns death to all living organisms, and then instills in the higher and more organized ones a passionate opposition to the fate she has appointed. Yet, though there may be various ways of making sense of this, saying that nature knows no distinctions is not one of them. At the very least, nature knows that life is better than death! We may be guided by the book of Genesis and the Gospels to understand life and death theologically as the imprint of our creation and our fall—but we do not need the book of Genesis and the gospels to tell us that there *is* an order of value in which life is preferable to death. We only need—just once in our life—to be dangerously ill, or to find ourselves at the bedside of someone else in that condition, and to wonder at the remarkable conviction with which we hold on to the good of life.

To take the step from a philosophy of nature to a theology of creation is not to abandon one set of interests in favor of another. The revealed purposes of God in creation will direct our attention back to *the world,* i.e., the totality of what there God has made, and teach us how to see the good he has given us within it. Any purposes God has in making the world are to be discerned in the world; they are not set apart from it somewhere else. Any discernment of how the world works will, pari passu, be a discernment of the purposes of God. No "presupposition" is required for this discernment other than that it is a *morally intelligible* world, a world in which there is good and evil to be distinguished, a world fit for humans to act in. All we need to assume is something that Adams, at any rate, is always quick to grant, namely, that the goods of this world are ontologically more basic than the evils.

What theology as well as philosophy must seek in the world are simply *the conditions of intelligibility of human life*, which is at once bodily, and therefore mortal, and yet "with eternity in its heart," transcending its bodily state and aspiring to all the goods there are—not only bodily satisfactions but moral recognitions, intellectual comprehensions, and even fellowship with God. To pose the question of homosexuality in *these* categories is precisely to ask about its intelligibility. Can there be any sense in an affection that appears to defy the logic of human bodily sexuality? Or is it not defiance after all, but a new disclosure of the good? These are questions that have to be raised (as, indeed, they are constantly raised by homosexuals), if we are to treat sexuality with the seriousness that the task of living a human life invests it with.

But Adams makes a different and unnerving move. A wedge is driven between creation, which is all about "beginnings," and goods, which are located in "the future." There are, it appears, purposes of God in creation. Loosely following the Western tradition, Adams conceives of three purposes that might be discerned in sexuality: a procreative purpose, a unitive purpose, and a cooperative purpose. But when we think of how these are to be fulfilled, our imagination is not tied to the way the world actually functions. Each of them, he argues, can be realized just as effectively in independence of the others, and that has the advantage of giving space for sexual partnership between what he calls "physical and genital" homosexuals. (The apparent conviction that homosexuality and heterosexuality are "physical," indeed "genital," conditions is one of the more baffling features of the argument at this point!) For procreation, it is enough that the heterosexuals get on with their usual business, or if they are unwilling or insufficient, the IVF industry can be stepped up. For the unitary good, homosexual partnerships are as good as heterosexual. For cooperation of the sexes, what is needed is equal job opportunities and women in the boardroom. All of which construes God's purposes in a purely voluntarist and arbitrary sense, detaching them from the philosophical task of understanding the goods of human existence as we find it. When the tradition spoke of three God-willed goods of sexuality, (offspring, faith, and sacrament, in Augustine's formulation), it did so precisely to point out the convergence of the three in one and the same natural institution. The point of the analysis was to account for the form of marriage as all human cultures knew it, not to reinvent the world. Once we separate God's purposes in creation from the inherent goods of creaturely existence, there is little reason to hold on to the view that God meant anything at all by making the world.

Creation narratives focus our attention on beginnings, he tells us, and though beginnings pretend to provide fixed norms, they cannot do so. Sexuality and sociality have changed, and change is only evaluated in the light of eschatology. How, then, are we to situate ourselves at the end of history, to evaluate it? Through "the goods God offers us to love." That is puzzling, indeed. The whole normative content of creation has been transferred to eschatology, moved out of the world we inhabit into a world yet to be revealed, *and then assumed to be immediately accessible to moral judgment!* Actually, the conflation of the good with the future is a confusion. Goods, as such, are not in the future tense; we do not predict them. Neither are they in the past tense; we do not narrate them. Goods are in the present tense, offered to us as the objects of our action, here and now. But we are historical beings; we live by narrative and hope; we grasp the present tense as set "between" past and future. That is to say, the present in which we live and act always has its two horizons, reaching back and reaching forward. We focus our attention on the good presented to us by approaching it through narrative and projecting it through hope. Christians have their own reasons for doing this: they have encountered a God who has made himself known as Beginning and End, Alpha and Omega, whose beginnings are a faithful token of his endings. They therefore speak not only of a good to be loved in action here and now, but of a good to be looked for in the future. But philosophy is not free simply to borrow the notion of a future good from Christian faith and substitute it for the present good. Philosophy knows nothing of the future.

It is, of course, right that philosophers should speak as believing Christians. It is right that they should do their philosophizing in a conscious openness to theology. By doing both these things, R. M. Adams has earned our appreciation. But it is not good that they should confuse understanding the world as it presents itself with random elements of eschatological proclamation. The result of that will be a deformation both of theology and philosophy. Theology needs the philosopher's reflection on the moral sense of the world, in order to think seriously about the fulfillment of creation. For without the love of what is, the "new creation" is an empty symbol—or is it a clanging cymbal? New creation is creation renewed, a restoration and enhancement, not an abolition. Not everything that can be thought of as future can be thought of as the kingdom of God. A brave new world of cyborgs is not a kingdom of God. God has announced his kingdom in a Second Adam, and "Adam" means "Human."

One thing at risk in Adams's approach, as in a thousand less articulate and less measured approaches along the same path, is the disappearance of scientific knowledge from the criteria of moral responsibility. We are invited to set the observation of nature aside, to cast ourselves on novelty. It is, indeed, striking how scientific curiosity—inadequate, one-sided and inconclusive as much of it may have been—has come to be banished from the discussion of homosexuality. Adams has done us the service of displaying the intellectual underpinnings of this development: a concept of value that has parted company with a concept of reality, a division between the good and the real. But moral responsibility to the real is precisely what the dialectic of creation and redemption in Christian theology safeguarded. Intellectually the outcome is curious and a little depressing: not only the approximations of medicine and psychology, but even the cultural-philosophical legacies of a Foucault—hardly a defender of the traditional view of created goods, but resolutely interested in the complicated constructions of human culture—disappear over the edge of an increasingly moralistic public discussion of the gay phenomenon.

It would be ungrateful to leave our critique at that point. For Professor Adams has a final turn to make, which may, after all, really prove helpful. From the notion of the good as future he steps back, in a kind of gracious retreat, into speaking of the good as "vocation." A vocation is not a future; it is a future horizon to which we respond in the present, and it corresponds to a past horizon expressed in the idea of an agent or a situation that has summoned us. "God *has* called me," we say, "that I *may* do, or be, this special thing." Now, vocation cannot provide a comprehensible idea of the good on its own. To appreciate its contribution, we have to tie it back into the goods of creation, from which Adams has apparently sought to cut it loose. A "vocation" is a *special* calling to a *distinct* good, different from that to which others are called. It is a distinct path of human action, offered to this person or that, but not to all. It is not a vocation to love one's neighbor; it is not a vocation to refrain from stealing; these are commands that apply to all. But it may be a vocation to serve the community by writing novels or driving buses. And it is an obvious question to raise in the face of any strikingly distinct line of conduct, whether it can be understood as a special vocation. The answer will depend on how and to what extent it can be a true way of realizing goods that are for all humankind. We may sensibly talk of the vocation of a Goya or a Bosch to depict the horrific and the disturbing in their art; we may not sensibly talk of a vocation of a Hitler or an Attila to realize the horrific and the disturbing in their military endeavors. Why this distinction? Because artistic representation can benefit us simply by expanding our imaginations; warfare can only serve us as it is kept within the constraints of justice and directed to the end of peace. The distinction turns upon what it is to be human. A vocation, which necessarily departs from the general rule, needs to be recognizable as a *human* form of service to the human community. How this observation may help open up the question of homosexuality is something to which we must turn in the seventh and last of our "sermons on the subject of the day."

7 GOOD NEWS *for the* GAY CHRISTIAN?

He will feed his flock like a shepherd, he will gather the lambs in his arms, he will carry them in his bosom, and gently lead those that are with young.

(Isa 40:11)

IN A THOUGHTFUL response to the *St Andrew's Day Statement* of 1996, Rowan Williams asked how the authors might address "the good news" to a certain type of homosexual Christian for whom he had a special concern.[1] Speaking in the first person, this Christian (to whom we shall assign the masculine pronoun) declares: (i) that he desires to live in obedience to Christ; (ii) that he is unable to see himself reflected in the description of homosexuals in Romans 1, since he is not "rejecting something I know in the depths of my being";[2]

---

1. For the text of the "St. Andrew's Day Statement," see Bradshaw, *Way Forward?* 5–11; for Rowan Williams's response, see Williams, "Knowing Myself," 12–19.

2. Williams "Knowing Myself," 17.

(iii) that he conducts a life of moral struggle like other Christians; and (iv) that it is "hard to hear good news" from a church that insists his condition is spiritually compromised.[3] This question frames very neatly the challenge the church faces. We may wonder whether the Archbishop's ideal homosexual Christian is idealized. We may wonder whether he is typical. But doubts of this kind are no reason to refuse the challenge. If there are homosexual Christians who see themselves in this way, then, precisely because they intend to take the disciplines of the Christian life with perfect seriousness, we may and must listen and speak to them with perfect seriousness about the good news in Jesus Christ. However, there is another question that ought to be raised alongside the first, and addressed to anyone who sees him- or herself in this portrait of the homosexual Christian. To raise this second question is not to evade the first; rather, it is to search out the shape that an answer to the first must take. This second question, too, is put by Rowan Williams: "How does the homosexually inclined person show Christ to the world?"[4] For if the gay Christian is to be addressed as a believer and a disciple, a recipient of the good news, he has also to be addressed as a potential evangelist. But we must take this second question a little further. The good news meant for the human race is meant for the church, too. What good news does the gay Christian have to bring to the church?

There is an elementary point about Christian ethics that I have sought to emphasize ever since the opening pages of my *Resurrection and Moral Order* published twenty years ago: there is no Christian ethics that is not "evangelical," i.e., good

3. Ibid.
4. Ibid., 18.

news.[5] There can be no change of voice, no shift of mood, between God's word of forgiveness and his word of demand, no
obedience-without-gift, no gift-without-obedience. The gift
and the obedience are in fact one and the same. They are the
righteousness of Jesus Christ, encompassing and transforming
our own lives, past, present, and future. To preach the good
news, then, is precisely what we do in expounding Christian
ethics, if we expound Christian ethics faithfully. Preaching the
good news is the only form of address of which the Christian
church as such is capable, whether speaking to Christians or to
non-Christians. When we use any other form of argument—
quoting opinion-poll statistics, for example, or reporting the
result of scientific experiments, or suggesting some practical
compromise—the relevance of what we say depends on how
well it is formed to serve the evangelical message. If the church
speaks not as witness to God's saving work but as a pundit or a
broker of some deal, it speaks out of character.

Yet to preach the gospel, whether to Christians or non-
Christians, is not a simple matter of offering reassurance and
comfort. The gospel, too, has its "hard words." The righteousness
of Jesus Christ is not comfort without demand, any more than
it is demand without comfort. It is never less than that *demanding comfort* by which God makes more of us than we thought
it possible to become. And from this there seems to follow an
important implication: the gospel must be preached to the gay
Christian on precisely the same terms that it is preached to any
other person. "The 'hard words' theology is given to speak,"
as Jean-Yves Lacoste has written, "are still words of salvation,
meant for mankind *as* mankind, not as Jew or Greek."[6] This

5. O'Donovan, *Resurrection and Moral Order*, 11–30.
6. Lacoste, "More Haste, Less Speed in Theology," 275.

should not be unwelcome to a gay Christian. What, after all, would it mean if we set gays aside from the bulk of humankind, offering them some special reassurance not meant for the children of Adam and Eve?

This was the point that the authors of the *St Andrews Day Statement* made when they wrote: "We must be on guard . . . against constructing any other ground for our identities than the redeemed humanity given us in [Christ]." These words met with a somewhat unsympathetic response. Either they seemed too obvious to be necessary, or they seemed too arbitrarily restrictive. From either point of view, it could be thought that the authors had some obscure polemical intent in writing them. What they had in view, in fact, was simply to assert the theological ground of human solidarity in creation, fall, and redemption, embracing gay and non-gay alike. If anyone thinks *that* point too obvious to mention, notice the range of inhuman views freely attributed by liberal polemicists to their opponents, as well as the range of "posthuman" views freely advocated by postliberals![7] Homosexuality is not the determining factor in any human being's existence; therefore it cannot be the determining factor in the way we treat a human being, and should not be the determining factor in the way a human being treats him- or herself. Gays are children of Adam and Eve, brothers and sisters of Christ. There is no other foundation laid than that. "He will feed his flock like a shepherd"; from which it follows, *simpliciter* and without adjustment, that he will feed gays like a shepherd, too.

Yet, it can be replied, there are other, less fundamental senses to the concept of "identity." Can we not speak of a "homosexual identity" in this less fundamental way, as we might

7. Cf. Waters, *From Human to Posthuman.*

speak, without denying anything in human solidarity, of a racial identity or of a class identity? And may we not ask how the good news may be addressed specifically to it? Since Gregory the Great's *Pastoral Rule*, bishops and other preachers have been preoccupied with how to address the gospel to sections of the flock with special needs—a gospel for the rich, a gospel for the poor, a gospel for the powerful, a gospel for the powerless, etc., etc.—which, as Gregory claims, "solicitously oppose suitable medicines to the various diseases of the several hearers."[8] I have to confess a reservation about this. I am not sure that it can be disentangled from Gregory's idea of the preacher as a *rector*, or "ruler," who safeguards and services a certain kind of Christianized social order built on role differences. Gregory's preacher strives to make role differences comfortable for everyone, chiefly by preventing them being overstated—excellent managerial sense, no doubt, but not the primary business of a Christian evangelist. The gospel is addressed to human beings irrespective of their condition, and there is no prima facie place to dismember it into a series of gospels for discrete social sectors. Why would there be a gospel for the homosexual any more than a gospel for the teacher of literature, for the civil magistrate, or for the successful merchant (to name just three categories that the early church viewed with the same narrowing of the eyes that a homosexual may encounter today)? It is for the church to address the good news, we may say; it is for the recipient—homosexual, pedagogue, politician or captain of industry—to hear it and to say *how* he or she hears it in and from this or that social position.

Yet there is more to be said than that. The gospel does have implications for the way we conduct ourselves in the world, and

8. Gregory the Great, *Pastoral Rule*, 3.36.

the way we conduct ourselves in the world is differentiated as the forms and circumstances that constitute the world are differentiated. There are special needs because there are special contexts within which the Christian life has to be lived out. Traditionally these have been discussed in Christian theology under the heading of "vocation." The preaching of the gospel can and must address distinct vocations, even though it must address them only in the second place, after it has spoken to us all as human beings, not in the first place. "He will gather the lambs in his arms, and gently lead those that are with young" (Isa 40:11). Let us imagine a gay person who has "heard" the message of the gospel but is yet unaware of any bearing it may have for his homosexual sensibility. Must there not be some *following up* of the good news, something to relate what has been heard to this aspect of his self-understanding? It is helpful to keep the analogy with teachers, magistrates, and financiers in our mind. Suppose a Christian teacher who has found in the gospel no implications for how literature is to be read and taught; or a Christian politician who has found no special questions raised by the gospel about policies for military defense; or a financier to whom it has not yet occurred that large sums of money should not be handled in the way a butcher handles carcasses. A pastoral question arises. In the light of the gospel, neither literature nor government nor money are mere neutral technicalities. They are dangerous powers in human life, foci upon which idolatry, envy, and hatred easily concentrate. Those who deal with them need to know what it is they handle. The teacher, politician, and banker who have not yet woken up to the battle raging in heavenly places around the stuff of their daily lives, have still to face the challenge of the gospel. Is it any different with the powers of sexual sensibility?

Of course, this pastoral train of thought does not entitle us to demand that the gay Christian (or the teacher, politician, and banker) should repent without further ado. Theirs is a position of moral peril but also a position of moral opportunity. In preaching the gospel to a specific vocation, we must aim to assist in *discernment*. Discernment means tracing the lines of the spiritual battle to be fought; it means awareness of the peculiar temptations of the situation; but it also means identifying the possibilities of service in a specific vocation. The Christian facing the perils and possibilities of a special position must be equipped, as a first step, with the moral wisdom of those who have taken that path before, the rules that have been distilled from their experience. A soldier needs to learn about "just war," a financier about "just price," and so on. Again, can it be any different in the realm of sexual sensibility? Discernment is not acquired in a vacuum; it is learned by listening to the tradition of the Christian community reflecting upon Scripture. In this exercise, of course, we cannot rule out the possibility that we may reach a "revisionist" conclusion. No element formed by tradition can claim absolute allegiance. But the right to revise traditions is not everybody's right; it has to be won by learning their moral truths as deeply as they can be learned. Those who have difficult vocations to explore need the tradition to help the exploration. The tradition may not have the final word, but it is certain they will never find the final word if they have failed to profit from the words the tradition offers. And if it should really be the case that they are summoned to witness on some terra incognita of "new" experience, it will be all the more important that their new discernments should have been reached on the basis of a deep appropriation of old ones, searching for and exploiting the analogies they offer. No one who has not learned to be traditional can dare to innovate.

If this gay Christian, then, directed to traditional rules of sexual conduct as bearers of help, complains that the good news is difficult to hear because his position is treated as compromised from the outset, he has misunderstood something. There is only one position compromised *from the outset*, and that is the position that is "revisionist" from the outset, determined by the assumption that the church's past reflections on the gospel have nothing helpful to offer. Certainly no one who sets out from *that* starting point will end up in catholic communion, for catholic communion presupposes a catholic mind. But the believer whom Rowan Williams introduces does not set out from there. He pleads that his purpose in life is "not just fulfillment . . ." but to become "transparent to Jesus, a sign of the kingdom."[9] He accepts, in other words, the *St Andrew's Day Statement's* point that discipleship cannot be without a price in self-denial but asks whether that price may not be paid, pari passu with the married, in the "daily discipline of a shared life." And then he asks how that daily discipline can fit in with its two exclusive categories of "marriage" and "singleness."

Two points about the Statement's appeal to these categories bear repeating.[10] First, the claim that these categories are mutually exclusive and comprehensive, covering the whole field of possibilities between them, is advanced on the authority of tradition, not of Scripture. Second, the Statement does not itself assert that "all who understand themselves as homosexual are called to do without such a relationship" (i.e., "exclusive, intimate and permanent," such as characterizes marriage), but says, "Some readers will draw this inference, others may not." A

9. Williams, "Knowing Myself," 18.

10. Cf. O'Donovan, "Reading the St Andrew's Day Statement." Also available online at http://www.fulcrum-anglican.org.uk/page.cfm?ID=63.

development of the tradition is therefore not ruled out, though serious conditions for recognizing such a development are stipulated. Further than that the *St Andrew's Day Statement* did not intend to go. Of course, no secret was made of the fact that the authors of the *Statement* approached the discussion with the assumption that the right category for the relationships of gay people was singleness, not marriage, and that this implied doing without an exclusive, intimate, and permanent relationship. But it was never the intention of the *Statement* merely to declare what its authors supposed to be the case. Its intention was to pose open questions to gay Christians that might elicit what *they* supposed to be the case. It was an invitation to dialogue within the basic terms set by Christian faith. The authors knew full well that other answers might be given to these questions than the answers they themselves would give, and they wanted to discuss those other answers too. They spoke to gay Christians as those who wanted to know, not as those who already knew. It had better be admitted straight away that the question-posing approach of the "St. Andrew's Day Statement" proved a communicative failure. It did not elicit the reflective answers to its questions to gay Christians that it hoped to elicit. Commentators, friendly as well as hostile, refused to take its questioning at face value, filled in the assertions they thought the authors intended to be read between the lines, and cheered or jeered accordingly. The strategy for opening dialogue fell victim, in fact, to the prevailing hermeneutic of suspicion. Yet I still find it difficult to conceive any other strategy that could ever lead to a process of mutual exploration.

Liberal Christianity has no need to ask such questions, because it reckons it knows what gay Christians need, which is, "stable relationships." Stable conjugality is the point at which liberalism has made its own peace with the tradition. Or, to put it more unkindly, it is its characteristic form of prudishness. There is, of course, a lot to be said in favor of stable relationships; but before settling on this as the decisive point, I would like to hear the question discussed by gays rather than by liberals. Is this in fact the key to *their* experience? Or is there something important in the roaming character of some gay relations? There is room here for a seriously interesting discussion among gay people which will be instructive to us all. What the gay experience really is, is a question of huge importance both to gays and non-gays. By no means everyone who speaks from that experience believes that marriage is the right model for conceiving their relationships. Some have seen it as the "bourgeoisization" of gay experience; and there are major advocates for the pattern of friendship. Such a debate among gays, if conducted frankly and in public, will provide the essential core reflection, helping the rest of us feel our way towards an understanding of the dynamic of the experience and a sense of how the good news may bear most importantly on it. If gays are to pursue this debate well, they will need to engage in analogical thinking, which is central to moral reasoning. They will need to ask themselves about likenesses of experience and about unlikenesses, about ways in which known patterns illuminate unknown, about the extending of paradigms to encompass new types.

Rowan Williams's hypothetical gay Christian, then, framed and posed precisely the question that we need his help to answer. And at this point, the author intervened, apparently in his own person, to sharpen the question: If you do not accept that homosexual desire is itself a mark of disorder, can you confidently say that the presence of this desire must always be a sign that sexual expression is ruled out?[11] This way of putting the question actually turns it on its head: instead of starting from given social forms, marriage and singleness, and using these as a baseline from which to reach out analogically to interpret an elusive and mysterious experience, it starts from an experience, and reaches out to posit a corresponding social form. Wrapped up in this is a certain psychological positivism, an unbiddability characteristic of romantic, pre-Wittgensteinian psychology. Within, we have a self-interpreting mental state, "desire"; outside, we devise an action to "express" it, i.e., lead the mental state uncompromised from the inner expanses of the mind to the public world. Inner certainties demand untrammeled expression. But that approach can only invite a skeptical reply. What is this inner certainty certain *of*? How can we know what the desire is *for*? The language of "expression" is treacherous. It lets us suppose that our desires are perspicuous, when they are not. Sexual desire in particular is notoriously difficult to interpret; the biblical story of Ammon and Tamar (cf. 1 Sam 13) is just one of many ancient warnings of how obscure its tendency may be. It is characteristically surrounded by fantasy, and fantasies are never literal indicators of what the desire is really all about, but are symbolic revealer-concealers of an otherwise inarticulate sense of need. But the point holds also for many other kinds of desire—let us say, the desire for a quiet retirement to a cottage in the countryside, or the desire to own a fast racecar. We cannot take any of them at their face value. "It wasn't what I really wanted!" is the familiar complaint of a disappointed literalism. To all desire its appropriate self-questioning: what wider, broader good does this desire serve? How does it spring out of our strengths, and

11. Williams "Knowing Myself," 18.

how does it spring out of our weaknesses? Where in relation to this desire does real fulfillment lie? It is in *interpreting* our desires that we need the wisdom of tradition, which teaches us to beware of the illusory character of immediate emotional data, helping us to sort through our desires and clarify them. The true term of any desire, whether heavily laden or merely banal, is teasingly different from the mental imagination that first aroused it. And gays have no infallible introspective certainties in relation to their desires that would put them outside the common human lot of self-questioning. "I became a great question to myself," said Augustine.[12] And it was the question of *himself* that the gospel helped him address fruitfully.

None of which is to accept, what textbooks and pundits wearisomely repeat, that a homosexual is someone essentially characterized by an inevitable homoerotic desire. That would be to close down the exploration of the gay experience with a vengeance! Neither is it to accept the equation, too attractive to some liberals as to some conservatives, of desire (or sexual desire) and sin. It is perfectly possible to think of desires as no matter for blame, and yet be persuaded that their literal enactment cannot be their true fulfillment. Think of the desires we conceive in relation to our enemies when we are angry, or of the desires we conceive in relation to money and possessions! Desire is, however, one aspect of what Christian doctrine used to speak of as "concupiscence," a brokenness of the world reflected in a confusion of desire that our human society itself instills in us. A recovery of the length, breadth, and depth of the doctrine of original sin would rid us of a lot of misunderstanding at this point. The gay Christian who complains that the good news is difficult to hear because his position is treated

12. Augustine *Confessions* 4.4.9.

as compromised from the outset could learn that it is not his position but the position of the human race that is compromised from the outset. The emotional resources with which anyone faces the world are a measure of the solidarity of human experience from which we have learned what it is to love other human beings in different relations; and in learning we are all, though in different ways, hindered. If the distinctiveness of gay experience reflects original sin in some way, it is because it also reflects the fractured quality of society and its loveless disorder, a disorder for which we all share common responsibility and all pay the common price, the fruit of our uneven social formation.

This train of thought offers us an insight into one aspect of the challenge presented by the gay experience, its novelty. The world has never seen a phenomenon like the contemporary gay consciousness. There have been various patterns of homosexuality in various cultures, but none with the constellation of features and persistent self-assertion that this one presents. And we need hardly be surprised at this turn in history if we reflect on the extraordinary discontinuities that exist between late modern society, taken as a whole, and traditional societies. To understand contemporary homosexuality without achieving some understanding of late modernity as a civilizational phenomenon is out of the question. But then, how can we understand late modernity without understanding contemporary homosexuality? Can we pretend to take a reading of the spiritual condition of our ultratechnological age without reading deeply the distinctive and novel forms of emotional experience that it has generated? It does not matter whether we suppose this society and its emotional forms will be short lived or long lived. The point is, they are of our day; they constitute a horizon of our mission. To live in our time, as in any other, is to have a unique set of practical questions to address.

If the first good news for the gay Christian, then, is that the "great question," the question of the self with all its pain and its hope, can be opened illuminatingly in the light of the righteousness of Jesus Christ, there is also a second good news. There is a neighbor with whom to explore the meaning of the contemporary homosexual situation, a neighbor who also needs, for the sake of his or her own integrity, to reach answers to questions which the gay Christian is especially placed to help search out. There is a neighbor for whom strict equality of regard and open candor—"irresponsibility," in the very best sense of that ambiguous word—makes it a primary obligation to put these questions and search for answers with a persistent patience not to be cut short by the concerns of purely managerial efficiency. The negotiation of soft and evasive compromises will not appeal to that neighbor, because the gay Christian's true self-understanding and well-founded self-acceptance in the grace of God is a matter to be safeguarded in their relationship as surely as the integrity of the questioning itself. One name for this open and candid neighborly relation is "friendship."

> But always to rigorous judgment and censure
> freely assenting, man seeks in his manhood
> not orders, not laws and peremptory dogmas,
> but counsel from one who is earnest in goodness
> and faithful in friendship, making man free.[13]

It is this open and candid relation that a liberal Christianity has refused by its managerial juridicalization of the gay Christian's claim, by its "laws and peremptory dogmas," designed to settle questions without exploring them, to adjust

13. Bonhoeffer, "The Friend," *Letters and Papers from Prison*, 390.

relations without justifying them, to reassure the uncomforted without comforting them, in short, to manage the situation. The juridical language of justice and rights offers the gay Christian a certain kind of recognition; the language of questioning friendship offers another quite different one. At the level of existential reality, the two are incompatible. The gay Christian today is therefore faced with a straightforward choice, a choice about the foundation on which he or she is to live. As always, the good news has a hard word in it: we can't have it both ways. The role of attorney's client, the perpetual petitioner before the court of pleas, is open and inviting, and there are plenty to welcome the gay into it—for the time being. But the catalogue of candidates for emancipation will be extended further, and the gay cause will lose the interest it once had—irrespective of whether it has won the concessions it fought for. The role of friend among friends, on the other hand, questioned and self-questioning, joined with those in pilgrim search for the new name that no man knows except the one to whom it is given, is an altogether different role, and perpetually available to those who seek it. The gay Christian thus faces in a particular way the choice that constitutes the human situation universally: whether to follow the route of self-justification or to cast oneself hopefully on the creative justification that God himself will work within a community of shared belief.

In this second choice nothing less is offered the gay believer than is offered to any and every believer: a role in attesting the work of God, in speaking to others of the redemption he has wrought. "How does the homosexually inclined person show Christ to the world?" Williams asks. Again, it is an obvious first step to ask why there would be a different answer for a homosexually inclined person than for any other person. At the deepest level there can be no difference. It is one and the same gospel witnessed to by gay and non-gay, a gospel of redemption from the enslavement of sin and of the purification of desire. Yet gifts are given differentially to members of the body of Christ; vocations are distributed variously to serve the common mission. Some are given in the form of special skills and abilities, some in the form of special opportunities, especially opportunities of special experience and suffering. From the place of special sensibility in which the homosexual Christian may find him- or herself, we may hear a testimony to the way the world confronts our mission in our time, to its fragmented identities, its disjunctions of feeling, its cruelties, its dislocations and the peculiar possibilities of redemption that God has put at its heart. The rest of us cannot do without this torchlight shone through the fog of the late modern world in which we, too, must grope our way.

What if the challenge gays present the church with is not emancipatory but hermeneutic? Suppose that at the heart of the problem there is the *magna quaestio,* the question about the gay experience, its sources and its character, that gays must answer for themselves: how this form of sensibility and feeling is shaped by its social context, how it can be clothed in an appropriate pattern of life for the service of God and discipleship of Christ? But suppose, too, that there is another question corresponding to it, which non-gay Christians need to answer: how and to what extent this form of sensibility and feeling has emerged in specific historical conditions, and how the conditions may require, as an aspect of the pastoral accommodation that changing historical conditions require, a form of public presence and acknowledgment not hitherto known? These two questions come together as a single question: how are we to understand together the particularity of the age in which we are given to attest God's works? And then the gospel has good news for us all: there is a friendship in which the most difficult questions about the self and the world in the era of time that is given to us can be explored and inquired into, a community in mission that can engage in the most difficult hermeneutic tasks. The good news preached by the church to the gay Christian coincides here with the good news preached by the gay Christian to the church. The content of that good news, perhaps, can be summed up simply by saying that the word "church" can achieve its proper content. The church is our neighborhood in the confession of Christ and obedience to his law, a neighborhood suffused with his love, a communion of mutual service and recognition.

The old-style liberalism that used to preside over the church's dilemmas in a confident spirit of practical compromise began from the assumption that everyone was divided from everyone else by recalcitrant disagreements. The Lord, the liberal prophets announced, had sent a perpetual famine of his word. We should stop asking questions of one another and hoping for answers, and eat the dry bread of commonsense compromises. Those who remember Pentecost may reasonably doubt that this was ever the wisest counsel for the church. But at the very least we cannot know whether and how much of a famine of the word there is in any disagreement until we submit it to the disciplines of patient common inquiry. No disagreement refuses to be analyzed, and its constituent elements sorted out according to size and shape. No disagreement does not lure us on with the hope, however distant, of a genuine resolution. Can we promise ourselves, then, that if the churches would only discuss homosexuality long and fully and widely enough, they would end up agreeing? Well, we are not entitled to rule out that possibility. But suppose it were not true; suppose that after careful exploration and a search for common ground, there was an agreement-resistant core at the center of the issue—a problem about how modernity is viewed, for example, or about the ontological status of self-consciousness; it might still be possible to set the residual disagreement in what the ecumenists like to call "a new context," and (who knows?) learn how to live with it. We have a parallel in the difference between indissolubilist and nonindissolubilist views of marriage, a traditional point of tension between Catholic and Protestant. That disagreement has not gone away; but if today it bulks less threateningly than it once did, that is because we are so much more clear about the extent of the agreed ground all around it—God's intentions for marriage, the pastoral desiderata in dealing with broken marriage, and the like. It no longer evokes threatening resonances. It is a problem reduced to its true shape and size.

There are no guarantees. There never are in the Christian life. But that is not a reason not to try. And seriously trying means being seriously patient. Anyone who thinks that resolutions can be reached in one leap without long mutual exploration, probing, challenge, and clarification has not yet understood the nature of the riddle that the ironic fairy of history has posed for us in our time.

BIBLIOGRAPHY

13th Lambeth Conference (1998). Resolution 1.10. "Human Sexuality." No pages. Online: http://www.lambethconference.org/resolutions/1998/1998-1-10.cfm. By permission, the Secretary General of the Anglican Consultative Council 2006.

Adams, Marilyn McCord. "Faithfulness in Crisis." In *Gays and the Future of Anglicanism*, edited by Andrew Linzey and Richard Kirker, 70–80. Winchester: O Books, 2005.

Adams, Robert Merrihew. *Finite and Infinite Goods: A Framework for Ethics*. New York: Oxford University Press, 1999.

———. "Human Nature, Christian Vocation and the Sexes." In *The Bible, the Church and Homosexuality*, edited by Nicholas Coulton, 100–113. London: Darton, Longman & Todd, 2005.

Anglican Communion News Service. "Anglican Communion Primates Meeting Communiqué." No pages. Online: http://www.anglicancommunion.org/acns/news.cfm/2005/2/24/ACNS3948

Bonhoeffer, Dietrich. "The Friend." In *Letters and Papers from Prison*. Enlarged edition. Edited by Eberhard Bethge. Translated by Reginald H. Fuller. New York: Macmillan, 1972.

Bradshaw, Timothy, editor. *The Way Forward? Christian Voices on Homosexuality and the Church*. 2d edition. London: SCM, 2003.

Breidenthal, Thomas E. "Disagreement as Communion." In *Gays and the Future of Anglicanism*, edited by Andrew Linzey and Richard Kirker, 188–98. Winchester: O Books, 2005.

Butler, Joseph. *Sermons: Sermons I, II, III, Upon Human Nature, or Man Considered as a Moral Agent*. Edinburgh: T. & T. Clark, 1888.

Church Board of the Church of Sweden. *Life Together*. 2005. Online: www.cofe.anglican.org/info/ccu/new/response.html.

Forsyth, P. T. *The Principle of Authority in Relation to Certainty, Sanctity, and Society: An Essay in the Philosophy of Experimental Religion*. London: Independent, 1913.

Frost, Robert. *Collected Poems of Robert Frost*. London: Jonathan Cape, 1943.

Gregory the Great. *Pastoral Rule*. In *Nicene and Post-Nicene Fathers: Second Series*, vol. 12: *Leo the Great, Gregory the Great*. 1890–1900. Reprint, Grand Rapids: Eerdmans, 1978–1979.

Joyce, James. "Grace." In *Dubliners*, 117–34. New York: Viking, 1967.

Hooker, Richard. *Of the Laws of Ecclesiastical Polity*. 4 vols. Edited by Georges Edelen et al. Cambridge: Harvard University Press, 1977–1982.

Kierkegaard, Søren. *On Authority and Revelation: The Book on Adler, or A Cycle of Ethico-Religious Essays*. Translated by Walter Lowrie. Princeton: Princeton University Press, 1955.

Lacoste, Jean-Yves. "Du phénomène de la valeur au discours de la norme." In *Le Monde et l'Absence d'oeuvre*, 109–27. Paris: Presses Universitaires de France, 2000.

———. "More Haste, Less Speed in Theology." *International Journal of Systematic Theology* 9 (2007) 263–82.

———. "Petite phénoménologie de la fatigue," in *Presence et Parousie*, 309–22. Geneva: Ad Solem, 2006.

Lambeth Commission on Communion. *The Windsor Report* 2004. London: Anglican Communion Office, 2004.

Lewis, Christopher. "On Unimportance." In *Gays and the Future of Anglicanism*, edited by Andrew Linzey and Richard Kirker, 149–58. Winchester: O Books, 2005.

Linzey, Andrew, and Richard Kirker, editors. *Gays and the Future of Anglicanism: Responses to the Windsor Report*. Winchester: O Books, 2005.

Newman, John Henry. "The Parting of Friends." In *Sermons, Bearing on Subjects of the Day*. London: Rivington & Parker, 1843.

O'Donovan, Oliver. "Reading the St. Andrew's Day Statement." In *Anglican Life and Witness: A Reader for the Lambeth Conference of Anglican Bishops* 1998, edited by Chris Sugden and Vinay Kumar Samuel, 38–51. London: SPCK, 1997.

———. *Resurrection and Moral Order: An Outline for Evangelical Ethics*. 2nd edition. Grand Rapids: Eerdmans, 1994.

Proudhon, Pierre-Joseph. *What Is Property?* Edited and Translated by Donald R. Kelley and Bonnie G. Smith. Cambridge Texts in the History of Political Thought. Cambridge: Cambridge University Press, 1994.

Rashdall, Hastings. *Conscience and Christ: Six Lectures on Christian Ethics.* London: Longmans, 1915.

Ratzinger, Joseph. "The Church's Teaching: Authority, Faith, Morals." In *Principles of Christian Morality* by Heinz Schürmann, Joseph Cardinal Ratzinger, and Hans Urs von Balthasar, 47–76. Translated by Graham Harrison. San Francisco: Ignatius, 1986.

Schürmann, Heinz. "How Normative Are the Values and Precepts of the New Testament?" In *Principles of Christian Morality*, by Heinz Schürmann, Joseph Cardinal Ratzinger, and Hans Urs von Balthazar, 9–44. Translated by Graham Harrison. San Francisco: Ignatius, 1986.

"St. Andrew's Day Statement." In *The Way Forward? Christian Voices on Homosexuality and the Church*, edited by Timothy Bradshaw, 5–11. 2d edition. London: SCM, 2003.

Vasey, Michael. *Strangers and Friends: A New Exploration of Homosexuality and the Bible.* London: Hodder & Stoughton, 1995.

Waters, Brent. *From Human to Posthuman: Christian Theology and Technology in a Postmodern World.* Burlington, VT: Ashgate 2006.

Webster, John. *Holy Scripture: A Dogmatic Sketch.* Current Issues in Theology 1. Cambridge: Cambridge University Press, 2003.

Williams, Rowan. *The Body's Grace: 10th Michael Harding Memorial Address.* London: Lesbian & Gay Christian Movement, 2002.

———. "The Challenge and Hope of Being an Anglican Today: A Reflection for the Bishops, Clergy, and Faithful of the Anglican Communion." Address, Convention of the Episcopal Church USA, June 27, 2006. Accessed March 14, 2008. Online: http://www.archbishopofcanterbury.org/640.

———. "Knowing Myself in Christ." In *The Way Forward? Christian Voices on Homosexuality and the Church*, edited by Timothy Bradshaw, 12–19. 2d edition. London: SCM, 2003.